William Spaid
November 1990

■ Naming The Mystery ■

Naming

The Mystery

How Our Words Shape Prayer and Belief

James E. Griffiss

COWLEY PUBLICATIONS
Cambridge, Massachusetts

Published in the United States of America by Cowley
Publications, a division of the Society of St. John the
Evangelist. No portion of this book may be reproduced,
stored in or introduced into a retrieval system, or transmitted, in any form or by any means including photo-
copying without the prior written permission of Cowley
Publications, except in the case of brief quotations em-
bodied in critical articles and reviews.

Excerpt from "The Naming of Cats" in *Old Possum's
Book of Practical Cats*, copyright 1943 by T.S. Eliot, re-
newed 1971 by Esmé Valerie Eliot, reprinted by permission of Harcourt Brace Jovanovich, Inc.

International Standard Book Number: 1-56101-016-2
Library of Congress Number: 90-37833

Cover illustration by Daniel Earl Thaxton

Library of Congress Cataloging-in-Publication Data

Griffiss, James E. 1928–
    Naming the mystery: how our words shape prayer
and belief / James E. Griffiss
        p. cm.
    Includes bibliographical references and index.
    ISBN 1-56101-016-2 (alk. paper)
    1. Languages—Religious aspects—Christianity. 2.
God—Name. 3. Language question in the church. 4. Liturgical language—English. 5. English language—Religious aspects—Christianity. I. Title.
    BR115.L25G76 1990
    231'.014—dc20   90-37833

This book is printed on acid-free paper and was pro-
duced in the United States of America.

*Cowley Publications
980 Memorial Drive
Cambridge, Massachusetts 02138*

Table of Contents

Foreword by Patricia Wilson-Kastner

Jim Griffiss has graced the field of systematic theology for a number of years. He has been clever enough to identify and write with clarity and candor about human knowledge of God. His *Silent Path to God* captured my attention because he articulated what may be the root problem of contemporary theology—the gap between prayer and theology. Furthermore, he offered some wise insights into the role of spirituality in uniting prayer and theology. Having in the recent past encountered colleagues who believed prayer was a device for clarifying our own beliefs and desires, and others who wanted only to feel holy before God and not think or be clear at all, I found Jim to be a great relief.

His new book, *Naming the Mystery*, continues his theological project of uniting prayer and theology. In this most recent work, with proper Anglican attention to Scripture and classical theology, he writes with awareness of our *fin de siecle* American culture. His reader is any theologically literate person who seeks to affirm heart *and* mind, our past *and* our present, tradition *and* creative future. Jim can engage wholeheartedly in such a venture because his theology emerges from a lively encounter with a God who is mystery. God is living, and thus familiar, accessible, and also surprising and new.

Jim reminds us that the living God whom we meet in prayer, Scripture, theology, and our present day world can be known and expressed in many and varied names. The church has known this truth for a long time, and is constantly forgetting it. Christians, especially theologians, can become either constant seekers after titillating novelties, or rigid defenders of theological systems that they venerate more than the living God. Jim seeks to offer us a theological approach to express our vision in old and new ways.

As a theologian Jim is open, receptive, and gentle in his style. That is no mean feat in a period that encourages us to call names and line up sides against each other. He is steeped in the classical tradition, but also well versed in contemporary feminist theology, liberation theology, and other movements that leaven today's theological dough. Attentive to those excluded from the classical theological enterprise—people of color, women, the poor, gays and lesbians—he does not idealize or absolutize their experiences or perspectives. His attitude is that everyone has richness to add to our Christian apprehension of God's mystery. Everyone needs to be heard respectfully and attentively, but no one voice should dominate.

Hurrah for Jim, I thought as I read on, for affirming analogy. He thus holds to a great and glorious part of our theological heritage, which enables us to assert that God is like us but not like us, hidden and manifest. Far too much of contemporary theo-and thea-logy is predicated on an assumption that if there is a deity, s/he is just like us, and perhaps even just another name for us. If we do not believe this, we are told, there is no God/ess worth speaking about. What are the believable alternatives to the new immanentism and its simplistic understanding of God?

Jim Griffiss rightly insists that good theology depends on our ability to comprehend that God is both immanent and transcendent. Thus we come to know God through a multiplicity of metaphors and analogies for God, which derive from the Scripture, our tradition, and experience. God has not one name, but many, all of which have some light and truth in them. If only those who cower in fear or lash out in horror at feminist theology, with its insistence on the inclusion of many different perspectives on God, could read Jim and take his theological approach seriously!

Because he centers his approach in Jesus of Nazareth, he offers a theological and religious focus for our experience of our world. Jim's Christo-centrism is not Jesus-olatry, but a recognition that Christianity is an historically rooted religion, rooted in Jesus of Nazareth and opening into infinite mystery. Jesus points us to divine mystery and guides us towards it. Jim's is one of the most balanced treatments of the role of Jesus in a theological system that I have encountered. Here especially I appreciated his awareness of feminist theological concerns, and his efforts to express Jesus' importance without the sexist oppressiveness which has alienated so many women from Christianity.

I hope that in his next work Jim can continue his humane and reverent approach to theology, and forge ahead with more constructive God-talk. In light of different modern critiques, the increasing participation of those formerly marginalized, and our own culture's growing search for the divine mystery, we need guides to help us speak our faith about God. My hope is that Jim will give us many more works articulating his inclusive, gracious, and prayerful theological vision.

Preface

Most interesting issues in theology are controversial, and this is as it should be. Frequently it is only through the hard work controversy requires that we can hear what God may be saying to us. Only rarely do theological issues involve intense emotional commitment to one side or another of a question. When they do, the theologian often prefers to retreat into his or her study and let others deal with the emotional issues. But if, as Karl Rahner once said, all important theology is *pastoral* theology, then retreat is not always possible, and the theologian must venture forth and take the risk of offending everyone by insisting upon examining both sides of a question.

The issues with which I am concerned in this book—our language to and about God—are both controversial and emotional. They require a willingness both to think and to feel, because they concern what is closest to our minds and hearts—God. I hope, therefore, that this book will be good *pastoral* theology, seeking to address the issues of God-language only to help Christian people in their prayer, worship, and service in the world. In the end, that matters more than polemics and scoring points against those we believe to be the enemy of Christian belief about God. In other words, my hope is that the book will "build up" rather than "cast down." Whether I have succeeded in accomplishing that hope only the reader can decide.

One of the great pleasures in completing a book is the opportunity it affords to express one's thanks to all of those who have helped in the writing of it. Many friends have helped me with their positive and negative criticisms—some with which I agreed, others not—but I have received all of them with gratitude because they enabled me to see the issues and emotions more clearly than I would have done without them. I want especially to thank John and Anne McCausland, who offered me many suggestions drawn from their pastoral and liturgical experience; Charles McCray, who encouraged me to write a book which people could read; Karen Wade, who "prayed" me through it; the students and faculty of Nashotah House who have borne with me during the writing process, and who have by their questions and comments helped me enormously; and several students in particular, who explained as best they could to a very inept learner the mysteries of word-processing, and who saved me on several occasions from disaster and despair.

I want also to express my very sincere gratitude to Cynthia Shattuck, editor of Cowley Publications, whose care, patience, and wisdom brought my early ideas about this book into existence. As all authors must, however, I bear responsibility for whatever faults remain.

Finally, I dedicate this book to the memory of U. J. Warrick, a friend and teacher for many years.

James E. Griffiss

The Conversion of St. Paul, 1990
Nashotah, Wisconsin

What Is Your Name?

> When you notice a cat in profound meditation
> The reason, I tell you, is always the same
> His mind is engaged in rapt contemplation
> Of the thought, of the thought, of the thought of
> his name:
> His ineffable effable
> Effanineffable
> Deep and inscrutable singular Name.

I t will perhaps seem odd to begin a book on naming the mystery of God with a quotation from a lighthearted poem by T. S. Eliot about cats, but Eliot, in addition to being a great poet, was also a very serious student of the Christian theological tradition.[1] It is unlikely that he could write about the "deep and inscrutable singular name" of a cat without having in the back of his mind the long Jewish and Christian tradition of the deep and inscrutable and singular name of God.

In the Exodus story of Moses' encounter with God, Moses asks God to tell him the divine name, but God responds obliquely: God tells Moses, "Tell the people the One Who Is has sent you" (Ex. 3:14). And from that story has begun the history of the divine name in its various translations and myriad interpretations: Yahweh, the One Who Is, the One Who Causes to Be.

The Jews regard the name Yahweh as so holy that it cannot be spoken. They speak the name of God, when it appears in the reading of Scripture, as *Elohim* or *Adonai*, or, in English, as the Lord. In many English Bibles, also, the name "Lord" is the most common translation.[2] The name revealed to Moses, Yahweh, is not a name in any usual sense; it is, like the secret name of a cat, the mystery of God.

Yet we Christians, and the Jews in a more restrained manner, call that mystery "God" and we do so, as Augustine once remarked, not because the word captures the reality to which it refers but because we have no other word to use in order to express so great a mystery. What is involved in using the word "God"? What does it commit us to not only in our lives, but also in the way in which we worship and pray and talk about what we believe to be important? It is a word that we use both to curse and to bless, to express the deepest meaning in our lives or to throw out as a meaningless expletive: "Oh God!" It brings with it a history as long as language itself. But it is a word unlike any other, for we cannot say what it refers to in any concrete or normative sense. It is difficult to locate it among the words which we use in our ordinary conversation—unthinkingly most of the time because we believe we know what we mean when we use words.

But for those of us who are Christians, the mystery to which the word "God" directs us must be named. In our religious tradition we believe that we can speak to God in prayer and worship and that we can speak about God in preaching and in our proclamation of the Christian faith to those who may not know or believe that the word "God" has any meaning. To speak of God and to worship God requires us to name the mystery of the God who is revealed and made known to us in Scripture and in the continuing experience of God that Christian people have had throughout the centuries. Because of our belief that in Jesus Christ God has come among us, we do not speak of or worship a God who is far off and unknown, a God without a name. We speak of one who is utterly holy and transcendent, the One Who Is, but who also is one who can be addressed by name, just as we speak to friends and lovers, or even to casual acquaintances.

Names, as we know, are very important in any personal relationship. Not to remember another person's name can be rude; it can even be an insult. I find it very difficult to remember the names of people to whom I have just been introduced, and so, even though I dislike wearing name-tags at meetings, I find them very helpful. I try to read the name in an unobtrusive way so as not to be rude to the person whose name I have forgotten or never really heard in the first place. However, when we are speaking of and to God, there is no convenient and visible name-tag pinned to a lapel or dress. We must look elsewhere to know the name or names of God. How do we name the ultimate mystery of all things to which the word "God" directs us?

In many Christian churches today that is a vexed question, one which is causing much controversy and pain for many people and much joy for others. The questioning arises from two quite different sources— the critique of exclusively masculine language about God, and the critique of western religious language by Christians in Africa and Asia. Both are raising serious theological questions. If we are to explore the question of our names for God, both must be recognized. The re-examination of our naming of God is not limited to the desire of many women and men for a more inclusive language about God, nor is it purely a feminist issue. It is a fundamental theological question about the nature of the God in whom we Christians believe.

In this book I want to consider primarily the critique of our names for God that has arisen out of a desire for a more inclusive language about God, because that is the most obvious and most pressing one facing the churches in the western world—even though, as I shall want to suggest later, the critique arising from those Christians who do not share our western heritage may ultimately prove to be of equal, if not greater, theological significance. Some western Christians, both women and men, I would emphasize, believe that the names which we have customarily used for God—such as Father, Son, King, and Lord—are no longer appropriate because their emphasis on the maleness of God distorts what we ought to mean by the word "God," namely, that God is beyond sexual distinctions.

Such a conviction has not always been the case, however. In earlier generations, most Christians would have said that the names of God are clearly revealed to us in Holy Scripture and in the historic liturgies of the church. And today many Christians would argue that we have only to look there to find out how we are to address God by name. Perhaps the names of God given to us in Scripture and the liturgical tradition are not quite as clear or obvious as those on a name-tag, but in the minds of many Christians they are there, given to us in the Bible and in the historic worshipping life of the Christian community. Many of the names which come to us from the scriptural and worshipping tradition address God in personal terms; they are names which usually derive from ordinary human relationships: Father, Son, Lord, King, Shepherd, and so forth. Others, which are more abstract—such as Spirit, Wisdom, or Word—are not as problematical. But those which are more personal have become problematical for many Christians.

Not only do some of those personal names emphasize the maleness of God, but others, such as King and Lord, carry with them a political and hierarchical meaning which is far removed from our more democratic society. Kings and lords do not have much significance today, so those names convey very little to us about the way in which God deals with human beings and how we are to image God in prayer and worship. They may even distort the nature of our relationship with God because of their historical association with political power and control. And, alas, there are some places in the world where cruel kings and wicked lords still thrive, even though they may not be called by such customary biblical names.

In addition, there are Christians in Africa and Asia who do not share our western philosophical and cultural history, but who do have a history and culture of their own. They too have begun to question the imposition of western European philosophical and religious concepts and practices upon them. Many of our concepts and practices have resulted from the historical marriage of a semitic, Jewish religion and the philosophy and religion of the Greco-Roman world into which Christianity first spread.

There are many examples which could be cited, but I will point only to two. The identification of God with the concept of Being, for example, has born much theological fruit in western thinking. It is a conceptual name for God, such as Supreme Being, which has its origin in Greek metaphysical philosophy, and it is one which has shaped our way of thinking about God and reality. Thus, in the Nicene Creed we speak of Jesus Christ as "of one Being with the Father." In order to make such a concept intelligible to a person who does not share our intellectual history, much interpretation is needed. To what degree are such concepts—for there are many others—integral to the Christian understanding of God and therefore to our naming of God?

At a more pastoral level, we western Christians need to ask ourselves how some of our cultural practices affect our image of God: the ideal of the middle-class suburban family unit, for example. To name God as Father conveys one set of meanings to people in a culture in which monogamous marriage has been the norm for many centuries, at least as an ideal. It carries with it a particular understanding of family structure—the relationship of the father to the mother. But it may convey a quite different meaning to those who use the term father in the more complex relationships of the polygamous family structure, in which our notion of the "ideal family" may be quite foreign. (Of course, our understanding of the "ideal family" is rapidly changing with the increase in single-parent families. I shall say something of the significance of this change later.) In other words, the critique of Christian language about God and the names which we use for God is not limited to the women's movement in the United States. It also involves how Christians in other cultures will speak about God. We need to see how a particular culture can shape our understanding of God and so also our naming of God. How are we to interpret these names for people to whom they are foreign?

When Christian missionaries first began to preach the Gospel in Africa and Asia, they assumed that those to whom they preached had no religious or philosophical history, just as many male Christians have assumed that women have no history or spirituality of their own. It was also assumed that the Christian revelation provided the only true revelation of God. Therefore they spoke of God and imaged the divine nature in language derived from their own history. In many cases missionaries even built churches which closely resembled those they had known in Europe. Christians in Africa and Asia, like women in the western world, are now seriously questioning the authority of the language which we western Christians use about God and the names for God which arise out of our way of thinking.[3] Both critiques—those arising from the concerns of women and those arising from the non-western churches—need to be considered if we are to understand the theological issues which face us in our naming of God.

The objections to biblical, masculine names for God, however, is the most pressing problem for those of us who worship in the churches of the United States and Europe, raising both theological and pastoral questions about human language for God. At the theological level those questions concern the authority of biblical revelation and the way in which Christians have both understood and imaged God. In a very balanced and judicious article (unfortunately, not all of the literature in this area can be so described), Roland M. Frye has argued that feminine language about God would result in a radical rejection of the biblical understanding of the masculinity of God, and would represent an acceptance of religions that both the Jews and the Christians rejected early in their history.[4] The Jews struggled against the fertility religions of the Canaanites, which worshiped the Great Mother. He quotes from a study by Elizabeth Achtemeier:

> It is not that the prophets were slaves to their patriarchal culture, as some feminists hold. And it is not that the prophets *could* not image God as female: they were surrounded by people who so imagined their deities. It is rather that the prophets, as well as the Deuteronomist and Priestly writers and Jesus and Paul, *would* not use such language, because they knew and had ample evidence from the religions surrounding them that female language for the deity results in a basic distortion of the nature of God and of his relation to his creation.[5]

Frye further argues that first-century Christians fought against gnosticism which, they believed, could destroy their belief in the unity of God by introducing a feminine dimension into the Godhead. It would substitute for the one God a hermaphroditic deity combining both male and female characteristics.[6] Frye's argument, and similar arguments by others, is a serious one and not easily to be dismissed. Even though certain feminine images for God can be found in both Testaments (for example, Is. 42:14, 66:13; Mt. 23:37), the preponderant imagery is masculine, whether it be as metaphor or simile—a distinction I shall discuss more fully in a later chapter. God is the Creator and

Father, or the husband of Israel, a shepherd and king, the Father of the Son. In Scripture and in the historical liturgies of the church, God is consistently referred to by a masculine pronoun and is never addressed as Mother. Frye and other critics fear that the introduction of feminine imagery into worship or the substitution of feminine imagery in Scripture will result in a new God, rather than the God revealed in Holy Scripture. It would also lead, he believes, to a denial of biblical authority in many other areas as well.

On the other hand several feminist theologians have argued that there are compelling reasons for introducing more inclusive language into our notion of the divine nature. Those reasons derive in part from the deepening self-consciousness of women in our time, making it difficult if not impossible for them to identify with a God who is exclusively masculine. Furthermore, some, such as Rosemary Radford Ruether and Elisabeth Schüssler Fiorenza, trace the oppression of women in western history to the systematic exclusion of feminine imagery for God in Scripture and worship.[7]

Ruether's *Sexism and God-Talk: Toward a Feminist Theology* is, I think, one of the best examples of recent thinking about our language for God. It is concerned with the theological questions which are finding expression in the concern of women and men for a more inclusive language. She seeks to develop in the book a new approach to Christian theology that arises out of feminine experience and the larger experience of men and women in the tradition of the church. She argues, as I shall do later, that it is legitimate to develop a theological point of view based on the experience of women because all theology has human experience as its starting point: "Scripture and Tradition are themselves codified collective human experience. Human experience is the starting point of the hermeneutical circle."[8] In order to define how the experience of women can be used theologically, she develops a principle which has been useful to many other women theologians: "the promotion of the full humanity of women. Whatever denies, diminishes, or distorts the full humanity of women is, therefore, appraised as not redemptive." The positive expression of the principle is this: "What does promote the full humanity of women is of the Holy, it does reflect the true relation to the divine, it is the true nature of things, the authentic message of redemption and the mission of the redemptive community."[9]

Lest this be understood in a narrow way, she is quick to point out that this is in fact a theological principle: "The principle is hardly new. In fact, the correlation of original, authentic human nature (*imago dei*/Christ) and diminished, fallen humanity provided the basic structure of classical Christian theology."[10] And she goes on to argue that the dominance of exclusively masculine imagery for God in Scripture and liturgy (as well as in the structures of the church) has prevented women from developing their own sense of God and of themselves and has indeed distorted the way in which men experience God and themselves.

> Women cannot affirm themselves as *imago dei* and subjects of full human potential in a way that diminishes male humanity. Women...must reach for a continually expanding definition of inclusive humanity—inclusive of both genders, inclusive of all social groups and races.[11]

At the pastoral level the questions raised by the language controversy have been a source of confusion and pain for some lay people and clergy, while for others it is cause to rejoice. Several denominations, especially in the United States, are seeking to deal with the problem of names for God by developing "inclusive language" liturgies or lectionaries,[12] but those have by no means received universal acceptance. One of the reasons for the negative reaction to such liturgies and lectionaries, of course, is the normal human resistance to anything new in patterns of worship. In the Episcopal Church, for example, resistance to the new Book of Common Prayer of 1979 was strong among many lay people and clergy until the changes became familiar and could be accepted. I can well remember an elderly woman who, when I visited her, asked me to pray from "the old Book" because she knew all the prayers by heart.

Yet for many Episcopalians nowadays the "old book" is the Prayer Book of 1979. Such a change in attitude may well happen with inclusive language once the new forms of worship have been used for a longer period. The prayers of all Christians may very well be enriched by a language about God which expresses the experience of women with holy mystery. On the other hand, one must also recognize that deep objections to the new forms of language and new names for God may arise from a basic intuition on the part of some Christians, the *consensus fidelium*, as it is called, that such changes are untrue to their fundamental beliefs about God.

What I hope to do in this book is to explore, both theologically and pastorally, some of the issues which are being raised by these controversies. My hope is not to solve the problems by offering solutions, for I think it will take much time for the church to see its way clearly in this new area. We must remember, after all, that the definition of the doctrines of the Incarnation and the Trinity, both so central to Christian belief, took many centuries of debate and political maneuvering before a theological consensus about language could be reached. Rather, I shall look at the theological questions which underlie the debate and so to clarify issues which have often gone unnoticed in the heat of the battle.

In the next chapter I shall examine first the context within which the naming of God must, I believe, take place and then look briefly at the two names for God which are fundamental to the biblical tradition: the name revealed to Moses—Yahweh, or I Am—and the name used by Jesus and the other writers of the New Testament—Father. But looking at those names as they are used in Scripture only raises new questions about the authority of Scripture itself, and how we are to name God out of our life of prayer and our experience of the world in which we live. Then I shall hope to show that the current questions are not completely new, for the naming of God in theology or in personal and communal prayer has always been central to the human relationship with God, and the nature of our language about God must be examined carefully. Finally I shall hope to locate the issue of naming within the larger context of Christian belief about the relationship of the world to God, especially as that is exemplified for us in Jesus, the Incarnate

Word of God who, as Christian people believe, is Emmanuel, God with us.

CHAPTER I

The Names of God

▪ 1 ▪

Once a distinguished philosopher, when asked if he believed in God, responded, "I can define the word God in at least ten ways. In which God do you want me to believe?"[1] The word "God" has become a name in Christian language; it is not simply a word which directs us to the mystery of all things. For Christians it is a word which names the one who is revealed in Holy Scripture and most concretely in the person of Jesus Christ. All names have a history. They conjure up for us the past, our personal relationships, hopes and fears, and the like.

When, for example, I use the name of someone I love, who has been of great importance in my own history, that person's name carries with it more than I would be able to express in words. It recalls to me a person. Similarly, the word "God" calls up for believers the history of their life, how they have been formed and shaped by the God in whom they believe. But even though it has become a name for those who believe in God, and is not just a word, it is a peculiar kind of name, unlike any other. It names something which I cannot taste, touch, see, or hear. Rather it is a name of power, holiness, and mystery; the name of one with whom I have a personal relationship, one whom I can call by name.

Sadly, however, in our time the name of God does not call up in the minds of many people one who can be named out of a personal relationship, or one in whom it is even possible to believe. To make the word "God" a name in such a sense is one of the chief responsibilities of Christian people at the present time, and it is really the crucial question which lies behind the present controversies about the names of God. There is little point in arguing and engaging in controversy about the names which we Christians use for God if the word "God" has little or no meaning either for those of us who do believe in God or for those who do not. Whether God is to be named in masculine or feminine terms, whether we use for God the pronoun he or she, is irrelevant unless the word "God," which for Christians has become a name, can speak with power.

Obviously there are many reasons why the word "God" does not seem to speak with power to many people in our time. It can be argued that in the so-called "advanced" societies of Europe and the United States, we have lost that sense of mystery and wonder which belief in God requires.[2] We live in societies which are dominated by technology, and hence by the assumption that all problems can be solved by machines and more and more advanced ways of controlling the natural order. Only when we are faced with major disasters do we recall, although fleetingly, that we human beings do not have absolute control over our lives and that we cannot solve all the problems which confront us.

One striking example, among many others, comes from earlier in this century. When the Titanic first began its maiden voyage, someone remarked, "Not even God himself could sink this ship!" When it did sink people were shattered, but quickly forgot that no machine is invulnerable to destruction. When there is a major airline disaster today, we are still shattered, but quickly pin our faith again on improvements in technology in order to make sure that "such a thing can never happen again." Certainly no one would want to deny the importance of technology and the contributions it has made (I am, for example, writing this book on a computer, which is much easier than using a stylus on a wax slab or a quill pen on parchment!), but we do live in a world in which the famous saying of Laplace, the mathematician and astronomer, dominates our thinking. When asked about God, Laplace is reported to have said, "I have no need for that hypothesis." Many people, Christians among them, live their day-to-day lives as though we have no need of "that hypothesis." All pastors, for example, know that many people who in their daily lives have no need for "that hypothesis" will turn to the church in times of crisis—when they realize that their lives are not in their own control. Sometimes that turning to God will have lasting effects; on many occasions, once the crisis is passed, they will no longer believe themselves to need God.

However, the problem for many today is a deeper one, an intellectual problem that has become sharply focused only in recent centuries. I think it would be true to say, although it is something of a generalization, that prior to the Enlightenment the notion of God was not an intellectual problem as it is today. Debates about the *nature* of God have occurred from the very beginning of the Christian era—over how Christians could defend their understanding of God as Trinity over against the absolute monotheism of Israel and Islam, for example. But there was not a significant questioning about the reality of God and of God's power and absoluteness. In primitive societies, the world was filled with gods.[3] Every tree and spring had its god, and each god had its own name. Gods were featured in myths, stories, and images that described what they were like and how they dealt with human beings.

As we know from the Old Testament, only in Judaism did the long and difficult struggle begin to move away from belief in the gods that filled the land to a belief in the one God who created and ruled all things, who was transcendent and holy, yet active in the history of the people of Israel. The story of the Exodus of God's people from Egypt through the wilderness to the promised land illustrates how the people came to see that their God was not the God merely of one place. Rather, their God called them out and moved with them and led them. The God whom they had known in Egypt was the God whom they knew in the desert of Sinai and in the land of Canaan.

But during that struggle and pilgrimage towards a ✓ belief in the one God, Yahweh, Israel did not raise intellectual problems concerning the nature of God. Her primary concern was doing the will of God, and of living in obedience to the Law and the prophets. God was active in Israel's history as a people, calling her to justice and mercy, not to intellectual speculation about the divine nature. These intellectual questions about the divine nature were being raised in another part of the Mediterranean world, in Greece and especially the city-state of Athens.

The Greeks, especially the great philosophers, Socrates, Plato, and Aristotle, began that intellectual pilgrimage which has radically shaped western thinking about God. They sought to understand the world as they knew it in rational terms and to arrive at a principle of intelligibility that would make it possible to say why transient and material things were as they were—how they could be understood, in other words. Socrates, Plato, and Aristotle did not, of course, arrive at the notion of a personal God, as had the Jews. They did, however, lay the intellectual foundation for the concept of God as a principle through which the world and moral action could be known and spoken about in conceptual terms.

It was not really until the beginning of the Christian era that both Judaism and Christianity began to deal with the questions that had been raised by the philosophers of Athens. They were required to do so because both Christians and Jews had to meet the challenges posed to them by philosophy when they moved into the complex cultural milieu of the Greco-Roman world. The Jews of the Diaspora, that is, those Jews who had moved out of Palestine and into other parts of the Roman Empire, had to reconcile their belief in the God of the covenant with what the philosophers were teaching in the great intellectual centers of the Mediterranean.

Philo Judaeus, one of the most important Jewish philosophers of the Christian era, interpreted the

Jewish scriptures in terms of the current philosophy of neo-Platonism. Through the use of allegory he attempted to show that Jewish belief in God was not barbaric and primitive, but that it could hold its own with the Greeks. Similarly, when the Christian mission to the gentiles began under the Apostle Paul, it became necessary to reconcile belief in Jesus Christ as the Son and Word of God with the philosophical ideas of those to whom the Gospel was preached. They did that in various ways. Paul, who was no philosopher, placed the event of Christ in judgment upon the gentile world:

> For the word of the cross is folly to those who are perishing, but to us who are being saved it is the power of God. For it is written, "I will destroy the wisdom of the wise, and the cleverness of the clever I will thwart." For Jews demand signs and Greeks seek wisdom, but we preach Christ crucified, a stumbling block to Jews and folly to Gentiles, but to those who are called, both Jews and Greeks, Christ the power of God and the wisdom of God. For the foolishness of God is wiser than men, and the weakness of God is stronger than men (1 Cor. 1:18, 22-25).

By the beginning of the second century, philosophers such as Justin Martyr, Clement of Alexandria, and Origen began the intellectual critique of religious belief in God and the revelation of God in Christ. They attempted to show how Christians could understand Jesus as the ultimate revelation of the one who is the intelligible principle of the cosmos. The ways in which they developed a concept of God have dominated western thinking up to the present century. From that extraordinary period of the church fathers and until the end of the thirteenth century, Jewish and Christian theologians and philosophers developed an intellectual

refinement of the idea of God. In the highly conceptualized and rational terms of Greek philosophy they
developed such categories as Being, Act, Substance,
and Person through which the notion of God could be
analyzed. And they were able to do so without abandoning the myths, stories, images, and symbols which
they had received from Scripture. The world and
human life could still be open to mystery, to the transcendent and holy, as the ground and hope of human
existence, which, as Thomas Aquinas said, all people
call God.

But we today live in a different world. The concepts
by which theologians in the past analyzed and spoke
about the divine nature have given way to the more
empirical world view that began to develop in the
Enlightenment. Now it is difficult to talk about God in
conceptual terms as Being, Act, or Person.[4] Furthermore, the critical approach of the Old and New Testaments that began to develop at the same time has
made it difficult for many people to hear of the power
of the mystery of God in the great stories and myths of
Scripture. The stories of creation and fall, of the Exodus, and the giving of the Law to Moses on Mt. Sinai,
even the stories of the New Testament concerning
Jesus—his birth and resurrection—are misunderstood
or dismissed altogether by those for whom the name
"God" is vague or meaningless. As a result, the awareness of divine presence, of a Holy One who creates,
governs, and transcends all things, is very dim. Even
though a majority of Americans, it would appear from
public opinion polls, still claim to believe in God, one
suspects that the word "God" connotes only the vague
sense of a deity who has little connection with their or-

dinary lives, one who certainly has no name that could call and transform their lives.

To a considerable degree this description of our contemporary problem with belief in a God who can be addressed and named in prayer and worship is true even for those of us who do believe the great stories from Holy Scripture. We too are influenced and are affected by the culture in which we live; our way of dealing with the natural order shapes the way in which we hear the word "God." It can prevent us from hearing in that word the awe of transcendent power present with us in our lives. "God" is a word which has for many of us in the western, industrialized world become trivial. It has ceased to be one that evokes a mystery and which calls us into relationship with the One who is, we believe, the meaning and purpose, origin and sustainer of all things.

It is within such a context that the current controversies about the names we use to refer to God are taking place, and it is the context itself which to a considerable degree creates the problems which we have. The real issue before us is not whether we call God "he" or "she" or some combination of the two, but *how the name of God can still summon us to belief.* The controversies, however, are important because they can direct our attention to the more profound issue: *What is it to believe in a God who can be called by a name?*

▪ 2 ▪

In previous cultures names have had a much greater significance than they do for those of us who live in the twentieth century. To a certain degree we are even losing our sense of the importance of names because of the increasing use of numbers—drivers' licenses, Social Security numbers— to identify human beings. But for other times and places, names were of profound importance. One of the first acts that *adam* performs, for example, is to name all of the animals in the Garden (Gen. 3:19ff). To give a name to a person is to locate her within the history of a people, to express one's hopes and dreams for her, and to call upon God for her protection and care. To know another person's name can also mean to have power over him and to know something about his inner reality, spirit, or soul. And for Christians, of course, the name which we are given in baptism is the name by which we are known to God.

In the ancient world, with its many gods and goddesses, this was especially true of the deities that inhabited local shrines and other sacred sites. To know the name of the local god or goddess was a form of protection: one could call upon them for help and use the power of the deity to accomplish one's purpose. The familiar story of Jacob in the Book of Genesis is one very good example of the significance of names in the Old Testament. Jacob wrestled with a stranger who appeared to him at night and demanded that the stranger tell him his name, thinking him one of the local gods. But he refused and instead gave Jacob a new name to express his new calling as Israel, "for you have striven with God and with men, and have prevailed" (Gen. 32:28). Jacob's new name, Israel, in other words, reflected and personified the transforming experience which he had with God when he was wounded in the thigh. Jacob was to go on as one of the great figures in the history of Israel—the father of Joseph and the forerunner of Moses. His name thus was of great significance for the people of Israel, for it told the story of Israel's encounter with the God of the covenant. The history of the people of Israel is conveyed by the name given to Jacob.

Elsewhere in the Old Testament the naming of God is of paramount importance, for it reveals who God is and the nature of God's relationship with Israel. The naming of God reflects the long struggle of the covenant people to overcome the foreign gods who inhabited the promised land. The amusing, but profound, story of Elijah's battle with the prophets of Baal is one example among many. When the people of Israel were being led astray to follow strange gods, Elijah said to them, "How long will you go limping with two different opinions? If the Lord [Yahweh] is God, follow him; but if Baal, then follow him" (I Kg. 18:21). In the story Yahweh proved to be the God of power and defeated the prophets of Baal.

Central to that struggle for the acknowledgement of the one true God in Jewish history was the story of Moses' encounter with God in the burning bush. In that encounter God is revealed as the transcendent one who would enter into a profound relationship with the people of Israel. It is a story which points to the heart of the mystery of God. The story as it is told in Exodus 3 is, as Bernhard Anderson calls it, "a superb example of narrative art...that portrays the divine calling and commission of a prophetic figure."[5] As Moses was keeping a flock of sheep after his flight from the Egyptians, he saw a bush burning which was not consumed by the flames. When he approached, he heard a voice saying that he was in a holy place and commanding him to remove his shoes in reverence. God spoke to Moses as the God of Abraham, Isaac, and Jacob, one who knew the sufferings of the people in Egypt, and as one who promised them deliverance. In the translation given by Anderson, the encounter between God and Moses is as follows:

> 3:13 Moses said to 'Elohim [God],
> "All right, when I go to the Israelites and tell that the God of their ancestors has sent me to them, they will ask me, 'What is his name?' and what am I going to say to them?"
>
> 14a 'Elohim replied to Moses,
> "I am who I am" [or "I will be who I will be"]
>
> 14b And he ['Elohim] said,
> "ehyeh [I am] has sent me to you."
>
> 15a Again 'Elohim said to Moses,
> "Thus you shall say to the Israelites
> YHWH, the God of your ancestors, the God of Abraham, the God of Isaac, and the God of Jacob has sent me to you."
>
> 15b This is my name for all time, and this is how I am to be designated for generations to come.[6]

There is much scholarly debate over how the name of God, revealed to Moses, should be translated, and even the origin of the word itself is obscure. As I said earlier on, for the Jews it is a name of such holiness that it is not pronounced in the synagogues. Rather the word "Adonai," or "Lord" (in English), is substituted for it. For Christian theologians, as we shall see, the name, translated in the Latin form, *Qui Est*, "the One Who Is," or "He Who Is," had a major influence upon the doctrine of God, especially in the Middle Ages.

There are three aspects of the divine name revealed to Moses which show us the mystery revealed in the name. First it is a name which shows Yahweh's history with the people of Israel. As the God of Abraham, Isaac, and Jacob, this is not a new god speaking to Moses, nor a god confined to a particular place or shrine, not even to the burning bush. Rather, this God is the God who was worshipped and obeyed by the ancestors of Moses, transcendent and holy, as well as the God involved with Israel's history—the God who named Jacob, the ancestor of Moses. Yahweh is a God with a history. Indeed, some biblical scholars have argued that YHWH should be translated not simply as "I Am," but as "I create," or "I cause to be what I cause to be." Thus the divine name can reveal God not only as the God of the ancestors of Moses but as God the creator of heaven and earth, the God, in other words, who is not self-enclosed but creative, the one who brings things to be and who is involved with all things.[7] It is thus not a static name, but a dynamic name, one expressing God's activity, not simply God's being or nature.

Second, God's name is revealed to Moses not simply for his edification, so that he could, as it were, know the secret name of God and thus have power over God. Rather, it is revealed as the sign of God's promise of faithfulness to the people. God is the one who will bring them out of bondage in Egypt. God is a God of the future as well as of the past. God is Lord, the one who is faithful and who will be faithful in future events. This is a theme that returns over and over again in Israel's history with God. God's nature is revealed in faithfulness to the promises which will be made in the covenant, not in abstract notions about the divine nature.

But the third aspect is the most profound. The name revealed to Moses, "I Am," is not a proper name at all. If we were to ask a person his or her name on a first meeting and the person responded simply, "I am," we should in all likelihood be offended or at least puzzled, because it is not an appropriate response. "I am" does not tell us anything about the person, except that he or she *is*. And yet that is the name that God reveals to Moses and is to be used for all time. God's name reveals, but it also hides. The God of the past and the God of the future, the God made known to people and in events, is also the God who is absolute mystery, the one who simply *is*.

As we shall see subsequently, this third aspect of the divine name is of profound importance for our reflection about God: that the God who makes known is also the God who remains concealed, hidden in the cloud of Mt. Sinai, or known only as a rush of wind. God is known and unknown, named and without a name. The God who is known in what God does is also the One Who Is. This *hidden, yet revealed* name of God, we are told in the Decalogue, which Moses later received in the cloud of Mt. Sinai, is not to be dishonored or spoken in vain. Such a sense of the mystery of the divine name persists very deeply in Judaism—much more so than in Christianity.

For Christians, however, the mystery of God's name, indeed the mystery of God, deepens in the New Testament. The name that Jesus himself and the authors of the New Testament use to speak of and to God is Father, while Jesus' followers began to speak of him as the Son of God. For many women and men today, the name "Father" is controversial, but it is a name that cannot easily be abandoned. Not only did it have a long history of use in Judaism, but it is the most prominent name for God in the New Testament and in the language of Christian worship and prayer. It has continued to be the primary name for God in the liturgy of the church, shaping and structuring Christian prayer and worship from the very beginning. We need to ask, then, what the name "Father" conveys to us of the mystery of God.

While it is not used in the Old Testament as frequently as in the New, the name is still important to the Old Testament understanding of God. At the same time its importance there, as well as its significance to Jesus, must not be misunderstood. Feminists such as Mary Daly and Judith Ochshorn have understood it as an expression of patriarchalism, the oppression and exclusion of women.[8] So it was understood also by Freud in his psychological analysis of the Oedipus complex in *Moses and Monotheism*. The figure of the father was for Freud a threatening one, a figure with whom a child cannot establish a relationship of equality. The father always remains a phantasm with which the child must do battle for the love of the mother. That family dynamic, Freud argued, was projected into the divine sphere so that God always remains a threatening figure, one with whom we must struggle in order to liberate ourselves and become authentic and independent persons.

Still others have argued persuasively that the meaning which the name has in the teaching of Jesus is quite different.[9] For Jesus the Father is the fulfillment and transformation of the fatherhood of God in the Old Testament. Robert Hammerton Kelly, following Paul Ricoeur, has argued, for example, that we can see in the Old Testament itself a growth and development in the notion of fatherhood. Initially the fatherhood of God was understood in terms of the father in the human family, one who was the progenitor of children, breadwinner, and ruler. But this patriarchal image of the father was gradually transformed in the history of Israel's relationship with God. The transformation began with Moses and in the Exodus experience of the people of Israel. There Israel was called into a new relationship with Yahweh, one which involved choosing and responding.

In our ordinary family relationships we cannot choose our fathers or our mothers, but must deal with both as a "given." In a patriarchal religion, based upon family structures, a people cannot choose their God. The god of a tribe is also a "given;" he or she is the god of a particular place or tribe. In many of the religions which Israel knew, the god was the father of the tribe in a biological sense—the one from whom the tribe derived through some form of sexual procreation. But as Moses was shown at the burning bush and Israel in the Exodus, Yahweh was not that kind of God. Yahweh was not their progenitor, as a human father would be, but a God who had elected Israel out of all the other nations, one who would bring them out of bondage, who had redeemed them (Ex. 6:6-8). The event which illuminates most deeply the fatherhood of God is the establishment of the covenant on Mt. Sinai. The covenant expressed the relationship between God and

Israel as one of free choice, not kinship, of loving kindness or grace.

There is an interesting parallel to God's free choice
of Israel in what is happening to many people today. In
our society many fathers are learning the difference
between being a father in the limited sense of being
the biological progenitor of a child, and being a parent.
A parent, whether father or mother, is one who has or
shares responsibility for raising and nurturing a child,
not simply the one who causes the birth of the child. In
one-parent families, the father or mother must fulfill
both roles, while in two-parent families many fathers
now assume much greater responsibility for the raising of a child. Human fatherhood can mean, and
indeed ought to mean, choosing to have a relationship
with a child that involves mothering as well as father-
ing.

Yahweh is like a parent to Israel, the God who cares
for the people as a father or mother cares for a child.
God adopts Israel freely, as a parent might adopt a
child. The covenant relationship breaks the sexual
bonding between Israel and God; it establishes a new
relationship of loving kindness and grace. It may well
be that as we in our present social situation come to
understand and experience parenting as involving
both father and mother, we may be able to appreciate
both dimensions in God and so be able use both names
more comfortably. All children have problems with
their fathers and mothers. As we grow up emotionally
we need to relate to our parents as persons in their
own right, those with whom we can establish a relationship of love and care, not fear and submission. It is
in such a sense that we ought to understand the name

Father as it was used by Jesus in the New Testament. For both the Old and New Testaments, Father is not a term which refers to God's masculinity but rather to the parenting care of God for Israel.

It is clear in the teaching of Jesus that the name Father is fundamentally related to God's rule over the whole of creation, especially over all men and women. The announcement of God's rule or kingdom was central to the teaching of Jesus. God's rule would be the beginning of a new age, one in which both men and women would have a relationship with God based upon God's forgiveness, mercy, and care. The qualification for entry into the kingdom would not be sexual or social identity, but faith, repentance, and obedience. As Edward Schillebeeckx says:

> Jesus' *Abba* experience is an immediate awareness of God as a power cherishing people and making them free....Abba, the "God of Jesus," is the creator of heaven and earth and is Israel's leader, a God with whom "everything is possible" (Mark 10:27). It was to faith in this God that Jesus called men through what he said and did during his days on earth....[10]

There is, indeed, considerable significance for this understanding of the Father's relationship to Jesus in the accounts of the virginal conception of Jesus as we find them in Matthew and Luke. Jesus has no biological father. His relationship to the one he calls Father is based upon his calling and mission to announce God's rule. It is, in other words, a call into a new way of understanding what it is to be a man or a woman, one which is not governed by family or sexual identity but by faith and trust. The Father, for Jesus, is the one who frees people from bondage of every kind and who calls them into a new covenant. Jesus himself displays what God is like: the father who welcomes the prodigal son, the woman who searches for the lost coin, the mother who gathers her brood, the one who cares for the sick, who feeds the hungry, and who tends to all of those in need. In the actions as well as in the teachings of Jesus, God is revealed as the loving Parent, neither a God far off nor an arbitrary ruler, but as the one who is close to God's people. When the rule of God comes to pass all will be equal and cared for in the Father's love. As Walter Kasper says in *The God of Jesus Christ*:

> Thus we find that in the preaching of Jesus the application of "father" to God has the same basic structure as the universal meaning and ground of all reality. What is new in the New Testament is the concentration of revelation in the person of the eschatological revealer of the Father; through him Old Testament revelation is brought to its surpassing fulfillment....In the final analysis Jesus' message about the Father sums up the whole of his message in a most personal way. It is the answer to man's hope, which can find its fulfillment only in the unconditional and definitive acceptance of love, and it is the answer to the question about the ground of all reality, a ground which is not at man's disposal and in which he can share only through faith—not because God is distant but precisely because he is close to us in love and love can only be a gift.[11]

But the name Father as it was used by Jesus is still ambiguous. No matter how we attempt to place it in the larger context of its meaning in the Old Testament and in the teaching of Jesus, it still carries a biological or sexual connotation and overtones of maleness. For that reason, I believe, we should look, however briefly, at the continuing development of the name in the New Testament and in the later theological tradition. That

Jesus spoke of God as "my Father" and that he taught his disciples to pray "our Father" requires some interpretation, lest we distort the meaning of the name.

In other New Testament writings, the name Father really became a theological term as well as a personal name for God. It would not be correct, of course, to read back into the New Testament the precise meanings of the name Father as they were defined in connection with the doctrine of the Trinity at a later time. Nonetheless, we can see in the New Testament, especially in Paul and John, that the understanding of God as Father of the Son, and of Jesus as the Son of the Father, began to have a profound theological significance. That God is the Father of Jesus came to express in other New Testament writings the relationship that all human beings have with God, a relationship most clearly shown in those who have been baptized into the death of Christ and raised with him. The new family of God in the death and resurrection of Jesus is one in which the baptized are heirs of the promise given by God in Jesus, and inheritors of the kingdom of the God who is the Father of all.

In Romans, for example, Paul can write that we who live by the Spirit, in whom the Spirit dwells, and who are led by the Spirit are "sons" of God: "For you did not receive the spirit of slavery to fall back into fear, but you have received the spirit of sonship. When we cry, 'Abba! Father!' it is the Spirit himself bearing witness with our spirit that we are children of God, and if children, then heirs, heirs of God and fellow heirs with Christ..." (Rom. 8:15-17). This is a theme to which Paul frequently returns: "For as many of you as were baptized into Christ have put on Christ. There is neither Jew nor Greek, there is neither slave nor free, there is neither male nor female; for you are all one in Christ Jesus" (Gal. 3:27-28). Our baptism into Christ makes us the children of God and enables us to call God Abba. It ends all those distinctions which divide human beings from one another. The Fatherhood of God and the Sonship of Jesus thus express and are signs of the humanity into which all of us are called in the one who is the Son of the Father.

The Gospel of John, which is also a theological reflection upon the relation of the Father and the Son, became a major source for the church's continuing use of the name Father for God. In Paul "Father" speaks of our salvation in Jesus Christ, but in John that theme is deepened and expanded. Jesus is not only the savior, but he is also the one who reveals God to us. In the prologue to the Fourth Gospel, for example, Jesus is identified with the eternal Word, or Logos of God, and it is through Jesus that those who believe in his name are shown the Father. "And the Word became flesh and dwelt among us, full of grace and truth; we have beheld his glory, glory as of the only Son from the Father" (John 1:14).

The same theme is developed more fully later in the gospel, when Jesus identifies himself with the Father: "I and the Father are one" (10:30), and "He who has seen me has seen the Father" (14:9). Indeed it was the accusation that Jesus called God his Father, thus making himself equal with God, which was one of the reasons for his rejection by the Jews of his time (5:17-18). In a passage which reminds us of the name of God revealed to Moses, I Am, Jesus responds to a question from his accusers in a truly startling manner. He had taught that anyone who keeps his word will never see death, to which the Jews replied that Abraham, the father of Israel, had died. To say that those who keep his word would not die meant to them that Jesus had a demon. Jesus responded:

> "If I glorify myself, my glory is nothing; it is my Father who glorifies me, of whom you say that he is your God. But you have not known him; I know him. If I said, I do not know him, I should be a liar like you; but I do know him and I keep his word. Your father Abraham rejoiced that he was to see my day; he saw it and was glad." The Jews then said to him, "You are not yet fifty years old, and have you seen Abraham?" Jesus said to them, "Truly, truly, I say to you, before Abraham was, I am" (8:54-58).

Jesus, the Word made flesh, is thus the one who reveals the Father to us. He is the image of the Father through whom we can know God and enter into relationship with God. John, perhaps more deeply than any other writer in the New Testament, saw the theological significance of the name which Jesus had used to express his relationship to God.

During the next several centuries, as Christians continued to reflect upon what had been made known to them in their experience of Jesus, those sayings led the church to develop the doctrine of the Trinity. If Jesus is the one who saves us and reveals God to us, and if in Scripture he is called the Son of the Father, then how are we to understand the relationship between the Father and the Son?

At first the two names (along with the Holy Spirit) were used simply as part of the received liturgical tradition. Following the commandment of Jesus to his disciples after the resurrection, the church baptized converts in the "name of the Father and of the Son and of the Holy Spirit" (Mt. 28:19).[12] But by the fourth century controversies arose which reflected an ambiguity in the names Father and Son—ambiguities which are similar to those with which we are dealing today. The problem was Arianism—a theological movement which argued that if the Son was begotten of the Father, then the Son must be a creation of the Father and not really one with God. In other words, the Arians were taking the Father/Son relationship in a human way: if the Father begets the Son as a human father begets his son, then the Son is inferior or subordinate to the Father. By arguing in this way the Arians were moving away from the biblical understanding of the Fatherhood of God as a freely chosen covenant relationship with the people of Israel.

The Council of Nicea in 321 sought to resolve the Arian controversy by *interpreting* the names Father and Son in biblical and philosophical terms. In order to remove any ambiguity, the Nicene Creed stated that the Son is "eternally begotten of the Father" and that the Son is of "one being with the Father." It eliminated any sexual interpretation of the Father/Son relationship. An eternally begotten Son cannot be understood in sexual terms: human fathers do not "eternally beget" their sons. Nor can a Son who is of "one being" with his Father be understood in human terms, for a human son is always different from the one who begets him. Obviously the name Father, which expresses most deeply and reverently the relationship which Jesus believed he had to God, requires further interpretation if it is to have any meaning for us today.

▪ 3 ▪

These two names for God—I Am, or Yahweh, and Father—are central to the biblical tradition. They interpret who God is, and what we mean when we use the word "God," in the most profound way. These names come to us with the authority of the two central figures of the Bible, Moses and Jesus, whose experiences of God shaped and formed Jewish and Christian belief and language. They not only direct us to the God who, as ultimate mystery, is hidden from us, the God who is without a name in any proper sense, but they also bring us into relationship with the God whose self-disclosure in Jesus Christ enables human beings to speak of and pray to that holy mystery. In other words, they point to the mystery of God as one who can never be fully comprehended by us in this life, but who is one who comes to us in the Incarnation of the Son and Logos.

But in considering these names it is important to remember that both names, given to us in the Bible, have been the subject of much distortion. When, for example, the Christian community first moved out of its Palestinian homeland and began its mission to the Greco-Roman world, it soon saw the imperative of interpreting the Gospel to a culture which had very little understanding of Christianity's Jewish roots. In subsequent centuries, the name "I Am" from the Old Testament enabled Christian theologians, who were themselves inheritors of the Greek philosophical tradition, to articulate with greater clarity the philosophical implications of the Christian faith.

Such an apologetic task was essential then, and it continues to be essential now, if the church is to communicate the Gospel in a rational way to those who may not understand and respond to religious imagery. The revealed name of God, which comes to us from the Old Testament, needs always to be interpreted so that it can clarify rather than distort what we Christians believe about God. There is always, I believe, a double temptation when we speak of God. On the one hand we can assume that "everybody" knows what the word "God" means, which is certainly not true. On the other hand we can speak of God in terms which are meaningless or misleading—that God is some kind of cosmic policeman and CEO, a professor giving us pass/fail grades, or a kindly grandfather who will give us anything we want.[13] The interaction between biblical revelation and philosophical, intellectual concepts, which began in the first centuries of the Christian mission, always requires us to interpret and clarify what we believe.

The philosophical interpretation of the Old Testament name for God, I Am, has at times led to the notion of God as a transcendent being who is impassive, far removed from human concerns—the "God of the philosophers," as Pascal called it. That misinterpretation always needs to be corrected, although I shall argue in a later chapter that the conceptual interpretation of the revealed names of God is always necessary, lest Christian belief about God be seen by others as wishful thinking or dangerous ideology.[14] The other biblical name for God, "Father," has also become problematical for many Christians. It is seen by many women and men to image God in a manner that cannot speak to their own personal experience, and as a symbol of much that is wrong in our society.[15]

In this first chapter I have argued for the authority of the two central, revealed names of God in the biblical tradition. We cannot simply abandon them, but they require continuing interpretation. Only then will they continue to express to us the nature of God in whom we believe: the God who is revealed to us yet who always remains incomprehensible to us as absolute mystery; the God who calls us to belief in the final meaning of all things yet who remains hidden from us; the God with whom we can speak as a friend yet whose ways and purposes are often unknown to us. Naming the mystery, then, requires of us a theological task, namely, to ask the question: How can we understand what we are doing when we name God? Such a task requires an exploration of the foundations of all our speaking about God as that speaking and naming arises out of our experience of God. It is to that task I should like to turn in the next several chapters.

CHAPTER II
The Authority of Names

▪ 1 ▪

I n the last chapter I began to lay a foundation for exploring the theological questions now facing many Christians about the names of God. Those questions come from two sources: the critique of western theology made by the churches of Africa and the East, and the insistence of women and men in our culture on a more inclusive language for God. I have argued that the two names of God which are central to the naming of God for Christians—Yahweh, or I Am, and Father—come to us with great authority, with what we call the authority of revelation. In addition they have shaped and formed much of our thinking and worshiping of God.

However, to say that those names have the authority of revelation and that they have shaped the theological and liturgical tradition of the church does not immediately solve all problems. Both the Bible and the tradition of the church need to be interpreted and explained in new ways for every generation. That process of interpretation is what the preacher does in a sermon: to preach is to seek to communicate what Scripture and tradition are saying to us now. A preacher does not simply stand up in the pulpit and read from the Bible, but tries to explain what a passage means and how it is relevant to the congregation. In other words, a reading from Scripture is *interpreted*. A teacher of theology does the same thing, attempting to make clear what it is that we Christians believe and how it can make sense out of our very complicated world.

While the notion that Scripture and tradition need interpretation is not new or novel, how each is interpreted can be a source of considerable concern. Some ways of interpreting Scripture, for example, would seem to undermine the authority of revelation; others would seem to treat the Bible as though every word in it is infallible, dictated by the Holy Spirit. One current example of both extremes is the controversy in some places over divorce and remarriage. It can be argued that what the New Testament says about divorce is totally irrelevant today and has little or no authority for us. On the other hand, it can be claimed that what the biblical teaching asserts—namely, that divorce and remarriage are wrong—is of absolute authority and cannot be changed. Faced with such extreme positions, other Christians believe that the church can neither dismiss the authority of the Bible nor follow it blindly. Rather it must try to see how we can address the problems of human beings today, while continuing to hear what is said to us in Scripture.

So too with the names of God. Do the names for God given to us in Scripture come to us with the absolute and unchanging authority of revelation, so that they cannot be modified, or are they simply irrelevant? If neither of those extremes is acceptable, then we must ask how the names that we use to speak of God can be faithful to biblical revelation and at the same time communicate to us in an authentic way who God is.

How can they be names of holiness and power for us today?

There is an eighteenth-century hymn that contains the following verses:

> Meekly may my soul receive
> All thy Spirit hath revealed;
> Thou hast spoken; I believe,
> Though the oracle be sealed.

> Humble as a little child,
> Weaned from the mother's breast,
> By no subtleties beguiled,
> On thy faithful word I rest.[1]

The hymn refers to those theologians and preachers, scientists and philosophers who would confuse simple Christian believers by pointing out to them the "subtleties" of the Bible. The implication, of course, is that everything revealed to us in the Bible and taught in the tradition of the church is clear and self-evident— somewhat like a blueprint. Life might be easier if such were the case, although it would probably be less interesting. The two notions, which figure so largely in the controversies with which we are concerned—revelation and tradition—are very good examples of the subtleties with which we are faced if we are to deal honestly and reasonably with these matters.

Revelation and tradition are not simply self-evident terms, they have different meanings for different people. In this chapter I will suggest a way of understanding them both that can also help unravel some of the issues of naming God. It is not enough simply to say, "God is revealed to us as a Father and the tradition has always spoken of him as Father." For one thing, as we have seen, the name "Father" is itself complex. But in addition, we must ask what the notions "revelation" and "tradition" themselves mean. Not everyone would understand them to mean the same thing.

■ 2 ■

The concept of revelation in the Jewish and Christian traditions is rich. In the Old and New Testaments, revelation fundamentally means making something known that formerly has been hidden from the minds of human beings. To reveal something can mean to remove a veil, to uncover and show a truth which is mysterious and awesome in its power. In the Old Testament human beings are not able to see God as God truly is, but the Holy One is manifested through various events, such as the burning bush, when God spoke the divine name to Moses, the pillar of fire and the cloud during the Exodus from Egypt, and the wrestling of the unknown God with Jacob in the darkness. There are many such stories in which God is revealed in some form of human experience or in a natural phenomenon.

God can also be revealed in the words which the prophets speak, "Then the Lord put forth his hand and touched my mouth; and the Lord said to me, 'Behold, I have put my words in your mouth' " (Jer. 1:9), for example, or the words God speaks through the prophet Amos: "Surely the Lord God does nothing without revealing his secret to his servants the prophets. The lion has roared; who will not fear? The Lord God has spoken; who can but prophesy?"[2] (Amos 3:7-8)

In the New Testament, revelation also means making known a secret hidden through the ages, God's eternal plan (Eph. 3:1-13, for example). But here revelation has a new dimension; it is associated with the person of Jesus. Jesus discloses the new age that has dawned, and he reveals what God is like in his care for the poor and sick, and in his forgiveness of sinners. In many of the gospel stories the writer is pointing to Jesus and saying, "This is what God is like." Jesus reveals God not only in his teaching about God, but also in his actions; he is on God's side, so to speak, and thus he can reveal God to us. Jesus reveals God to us in his person, that is, in *who he is*, not in asserting propositions about God.

Neither the Old nor the New Testament, however, raises explicitly the question that emerged when Christianity moved out into the world of Greek and Roman philosophy and religion. Pilate, a Roman, when confronted with Jesus, asked "What is truth?"—an intellectual and philosophical question. But for Judaism the notion of truth, and hence the truth that is revealed to us about God, refers almost without exception to God's faithfulness to the promise made in the covenant. Revelation—whether in the form of the Law and the prophets or in the person of Jesus—confronts the people of God with the demand to live in accordance with God's commandments. It is concerned with God's will, not with rationally coherent propositions about the truth of things.[3]

When, however, Christianity moved into the world of classical culture, ideas about revelation changed. The church was faced with a culture concerned with the rational nature of truth, often in opposition to religious myths and beliefs. Even before Socrates, who was the great critic of popular religion in Greece, the philosophers had seen much in popular religion they found contrary to reason and subversive to a true understanding of the divine nature. When Christians began to preach about Jesus Christ to the world of the Greeks and Romans, their apologetic task was to show that what had been revealed in Scripture, and especially in the life, death, and resurrection of Jesus, was not contrary to a rational interpretation of the world. This was a task they undertook with considerable intellectual vigor.

The early Christian apologists and theologians sought to demonstrate that there was no hard and fast distinction between truth as it had been revealed in Scripture and what could be known through rational inquiry. Both were in varying degrees inspired by the same Spirit of God and both shared in the Word of God incarnate in Jesus Christ.[4] With varying degrees of emphasis and occasional outbursts of anti-rationalism, this approach continued until the end of the medieval period. One of the great achievements of the medieval theology of St. Thomas Aquinas, for example, was his integration of what we believe by faith in God's revelation with what we know by means of reason. For Thomas, the revelation to which we respond in faith fulfills and completes human reason; it opens reason up to a greater mystery than reason alone could attain. While the authority of revelation is greater, it is not in opposition or conflict with what human beings could know through reason. St. Thomas argues, for example, that all human beings can know there is a God through their rational analysis of the created order.

Without revelation, however, they cannot know that the one God exists as trinity of persons.[5]

The conflict between revelation and reason that arose towards the end of the thirteenth century is the root of the problem we have today, as we seek to understand both the authority of revelation in Scripture and how Scripture has been interpreted in the tradition. In the Reformation period, for example, Luther could speak of "the whore of reason" because, he believed, reason deluded human beings into believing they could have a relationship with God that was not based upon faith. Rational speculation about God only feeds human pride and our ever-present tendency towards idolatry of ourselves and our own strength.[6] In the Enlightenment and later, with the development of a world view based upon a scientific and empirical methodology, revelation, as a legitimate form of knowledge about God, came increasingly under attack from those whom the philosopher Schleiermacher called "cultured despisers" of religion. As a result, those who still believed that revelation offered a legitimate knowledge of God and of God's work in the world developed a fortress mentality. The Bible was immune to scientific and historical criticism; it provided its own justification and needed no other authority because it had the authority of God.

Today such an attitude towards revelation still persists in many churches. There are television preachers, for example, who argue that the stories of creation, the origin of the human race, the flood, and such like, must be taken as literally true in spite of scientific evidence to the contrary. Those who oppose the inclusion of female imagery and names for God are by no means so simplistic in their approach to revelation, but they do approach the authority of revelation in a similar way when it comes to language about God. They argue, as we have seen, that exclusively masculine imagery for God must be preserved because it carries with it the authority of revelation. Some have also argued that there can be no tampering with the codes of sexual morality found in Scripture, or with the maleness of the ordained ministry, because both have the authority of revelation. In deciding how we are to interpret Scripture, often there appears to be only a fine line between those who argue for creationism, for example, and those who would maintain that exclusively masculine imagery for God, an all-male ordained ministry, and biblical sexual codes carry with them the unchangeable authority of revelation.[7]

My concern here, of course, is with the revealed authority of the names for God, but those other issues also require us to develop a way of understanding and interpreting the revelation of God. We must learn to interpret revealed knowledge in the light of that understanding we have come to through our analysis of ourselves and our world.

Revelation, Christians believe, is concerned with truth—the truth about ourselves, who we are and what we are called to be in God, and the truth about God. As we know from our ordinary human relationships, the truth about a person is expressed, or better, summed up, in a person's name. If I call a good friend by the wrong name, I have not spoken a true word about her; I have, so to speak, forgotten her. What is the truth about God revealed to us in the divine names? How can we say that the truth revealed to us expresses the relationship we have with God and so has authority for us?

Christian people believe that in Jesus Christ the truth about God, the world, and ourselves has been revealed to us. In the name that he used to speak to God, Jesus deepened the meaning of the name of God revealed to Moses, I Am; he interpreted it in the richer context of a personal relationship. In the life, death, and resurrection of Jesus, Christians believe, God is revealed to us as the divine parent who is faithful and who cares ultimately and absolutely for all human beings. God is revealed not simply as a concept, a rational idea, but as someone who is able to enter into relationships with us, relationships that are not imposed by force, but arise out of freedom and love.

Revealed truth for Christian belief is ultimately personal; it is neither scientific propositions, theological statements, nor moral codes. It is truth, made known to us in a human being like ourselves, Jesus. It is about the person Jesus and the personal God whom he reveals to us. Truth in this sense is a personal relationship into which we can grow and through which more and more is shown to us. Jesus Christ is the making known of God's eternal plan of redemption, the reconciliation of God and us, the establishment of the new creation. To use an analogy, we know that personal relationships like love or friendship always call us on, enabling us and the other person to grow into deeper understanding. It is not something just fixed, settled, static, and unchanging. So too with the God revealed in Jesus Christ. I believe that I can enter more and more deeply into the God who is revealed to me as ultimately personal.

Understood in such a way, the New Testament and
the Bible as a whole, far from being a handbook of
rules or a collection of unchanging propositions about
God, is the witness to who God is, now fully revealed
in Jesus. It witnesses to Jesus and his revelation of
God by telling the story of God's history with human
beings, and it begins the process of forming and shaping the doctrinal and liturgical tradition of the church,
that is to say, what the church believes about God and
how it expresses this belief.

Jesus Christ is the final revelation of God to which
Scripture and tradition bear witness. Only in terms of
the risen Christ, present to the church through the
Spirit, and the experience of Christian people, can all
of our language about God be judged. It is legitimate,
then, to ask: do the names we use about God express
the reality of the God who is with us in Jesus Christ?
It is clearly not enough simply to say that a particular
name is in the Bible. It must show us God by witness-
ing to the risen Christ and enabling us to believe more
deeply.

Here the feminist critique of religious language is
correct. We must bring to our understanding and interpretation of Scripture who we are as human beings,
what we have known, believed, and loved. Any good
preacher or teacher does that. Preachers and teachers
bring to their interpretation of Scripture an authority
which arises out of themselves in their relationship to
God—out of their prayer, worship, moral life, and reflection. As I shall show more thoroughly later in this
book, the authority of Scripture, and thus the authority of the names of God revealed to us in Scripture,
arises to a significant degree out of our life with God

and our life in community. It is not simply an authority imposed upon us from outside.

■ 3 ■

To think of revelation in the way I have been suggesting has important consequences for our understanding of the authority of Scripture and tradition. Whatever we may have to say about authority, whether of Scripture itself or as it is exercised in the churches, will follow from what we believe about God. Authority is centered in God and how God is revealed to us in Jesus Christ. Every church tradition—Protestant, Catholic, and Orthodox—has its own way of understanding how the authority of God in Christ is mediated in the daily life of the institution and of individuals. But the vital thing, which we must always remember, is that no institution can claim for itself the ultimate authority that belongs to the God who is personally revealed to us in Jesus Christ.[8]

In western society today there is a serious questioning of authority, not only the authority of God, but also of those institutions that claim to speak with authority. Both politicians and ecclesiastics like to point to several areas where they consider a crisis in authority to be occurring: the breakdown of parental authority, a lack of respect for the law, and an indifference to or rejection of "traditional moral values," especially in the area of sexual morality. It may well be, of course, that the perceived crisis is simply a time of transition from one set of values to another. That transition has happened on other occasions in the past, when new values led to a different understanding of authority—the gradual disappearance, for example, of the patriarchal family of the last century. If that is the case, then new structures of authority will eventually emerge.

For the moment, however, all of those areas are a cause of concern. In many circles the blame is put upon our failure to acknowledge the authority of the Bible. Many people—not only those who listen to television preachers or who belong to extreme fundamentalist churches, but also those in the historic churches—claim that a return to accepting the authority of the Bible would solve many of our problems. I once had a conversation with a parishioner that illustrates well that attitude even for the more "liberal" churches. The man asked me to explain to him how the Episcopal Church could even debate the issue of homosexuality, when the Bible clearly forbade it. And he asked for a response that, as he said, would not involve "any of this theological and psychological stuff." My inability to answer him on his terms indicates the problem. If the Bible, taken literally, cannot solve all of our problems, then what is authoritative for us?

The problem of authority in our society, I would suggest, goes much deeper than simply the rejection of the Bible as an authoritative norm or guide. In the first place, there is the questioning of the authority of belief itself. Can I—can anyone—really believe in anything whatsoever? Can I acknowledge any person or system which claims the authority of truth and moral obligation? Does an authority exist that can lay a claim on me not through its power to coerce, but through a relationship of mutual obligation, respect, and freedom? For Jews and Christians such a relationship is shown in the covenant between God and the people of Israel. It involves the recognition and acceptance of a reality that transcends the immediate desires and needs of any individual or community. This covenant has shaped the religious and political life of Israel, and the new covenant, established in Jesus, for many centuries formed Christian political and religious beliefs. Yet it is increasingly the case that the acknowledgement of any transcendent authority with whom we can enter into a relationship of trust and responsibility is seriously questioned or even ignored.

So the question of belief in God is ultimately the fundamental question of authority. It is the question that must be recognized, even if it cannot be answered, prior to any other. As I said in the last chapter, any discussion of the names for God is trivial if the word "God" is not a word expressing the power of holiness. Holy Scripture asks, and the church has continued to ask, how can we tell a true prophet or a true teaching from a false one? More and more we find ourselves asking, can there be a prophet or an authoritative teaching at all? The difference between the two questions is considerable and deeply important. It affects the way in which we shall understand the authority of God, as it is mediated to us in Scripture and the teaching authority of the church's tradition.

Most Christians, however, profess to believe in the authority of God revealed to us in Christ and in the continuing presence of the Holy Spirit in the church. For us, then, the question is how that authority is mediated to us. That is the question now vexing many of the churches, both Protestant and Catholic, as they struggle with the interpretation of Scripture, the question of the language about God being only one example. In the New Testament itself, we can see the different ways in which the authority of God made known in Jesus Christ came to be understood, especially as the early church moved out of its Jewish matrix and into the Greco-Roman world. There gradually developed various components through which authority was mediated: canonical scriptures, the ordained ministry, liturgical practice, and personal charism.[9] All had to be held together in tension; no one form could be taken as exclusively authoritative. When one component was taken in isolation from the others, errors flourished.

The subsequent history of the church provides many examples of what happens when the healthy tension of Scripture, doctrinal tradition, liturgical forms, and ordained ministry is dissolved. Protestants would point to the absolute authority in matters of faith and morals claimed for the Bishop of Rome as an example of such imbalance. Roman Catholics, on the other hand, would point to the exclusive reliance upon Scripture on the part of some Protestant churches as a similar imbalance. Today, as in the past, we must struggle to keep those various elements together as we are faced with new questions by women, by the poor and disadvantaged, and by those from non-western cultures. The question for us is one of authority: how can the authority of Christ be mediated to Christian people through the Spirit in regard to the questions that such groups are raising?

In order to answer that question I want to put forward three ideas about the nature of authority in the church. Certainly, they will not solve all of the problems, but I hope they can enable us to see more clearly where we are going. First, because for Christians the ultimate source of authority is God in Christ, that authority is always *personal*. "God" is not merely a word; it refers to one whom we can address by name. The God whom we can address by name is present through the Spirit of Jesus Christ, present in the worshiping and praying life of the Christian community in every time and place. God's authority, in other words, is mediated to us now as we hear the words of Scripture, receive the sacraments, confess our belief in the God whom we can name, and live out the obligations of the Christian life.[10] God is a present reality to Christian people, not just a God whom we read about in the Bible. The presence of God *now* is one of the ways in which God's personal authority is mediated to us.

Second, the authority of God in Christ is known and mediated through Holy Scripture and the various structures, institutions, doctrinal formulations, and liturgical forms that have developed in the history of the church from the New Testament on. Both Scripture and those various forms, precisely because they are historical, must always be open to *critical examination*. No mediated authority can be its own justification; it always shares in the fallibility of human beings, and must remain open to further change and development. Even Holy Scripture, which witnesses in a primary way to the revelation of God in Christ Jesus, was written down by fallible human beings under the guidance of the Spirit. As such, Scripture requires interpretation in the light of contemporary knowledge and belief.[11]

For example, if the two names for God we have been considering, which come to us from Scripture, have so radically changed their meaning that they distort what Christians now believe, then they will need interpretation. As I argued in the last chapter, the name I Am needs much interpretation for those who do not share the philosophical history of western Christianity. Simply to use that name in an uncritical way could well distort our understanding of the nature of God.

The third proposition, then, is that the present experience of Christian people must always be checked against the norms of Scripture and tradition, lest we stray too far from the witness they bear to Christ. As Article VI of the Articles of Religion says: "Holy Scripture containeth all things necessary to salvation: so that whatsoever is not read therein, nor may be proved thereby, is not to be required of any man, that it should be believed as an article of the Faith, or be thought requisite or necessary to salvation."[12] At the same time, the normative authority of Scripture and the doctrinal and liturgical tradition must be checked against the Spirit-filled life and experience of the believing and worshiping community. In a later chapter I shall say more about what it means to speak of the present experience the believing community has of God. But here we need always remember that to pray for the Spirit to guide and direct us is to acknowledge our belief that final truth, and hence the ultimate authority of God, is eschatological; we do not yet know into what truth we shall be led. Nor even do we know that the way we are following will always be the correct way; Christians live by trust in God's promise, not by the certainty offered in propositions and institutions.

So we can say that Scripture has authority for us for two reasons: first, it bears authentic witness to Jesus Christ by speaking a true word about God; second, the community that hears the word is led by the Spirit to accept its authenticity. Scripture witnesses to Jesus Christ authentically through the continuity between the experience of the Risen Christ in every generation and those who first believed. It is the continuity between the Jesus who was known "in the flesh" and the Jesus who continues to be known "in the Spirit," that is, as Savior and Lord. When we read and pray the Scriptures now, we are able to hear of the Risen Christ as someone we also know in the believing and worshiping community. The word we hear now enables us to respond in faith to Christ just as others have in the past. Scripture is not coercive; it speaks from faith to faith, and it speaks the truth to us that enables us to believe and know God's salvation. In and through all of the different strands, levels, and interpretations of the Old and New Testaments we are able to hear the Good News of God's saving work in history. For those who hear the Word in the words of Scripture, it proclaims a unity and pattern of truth. Hence no one part of Scripture can be taken in isolation from the whole. Each must be heard in the context of its relationship to other passages and themes, for each completes the pattern of truth that is the Gospel.

Such a way of understanding the authority of Scripture applies to the questions that concern us here: the names of God. The names used in Scripture must be understood in their unity with one another and with other dimensions of the teachings of Scripture. To single out one name, such as Father or I Am, and to claim for it exclusive and absolute authority, would be to ignore the unity and pattern of the fundamental images of God that Scripture places before us. We have many ways of talking about and naming God, some conceptual, others personal and imagistic. All those concepts, names, and images must be interpreted rationally and critically if they are to be authoritative for us.

Scripture, then, is authoritative and normative for the church. Even though written by fallible human beings, it stands over the church in judgment because of its power to recall it to its foundation in Jesus Christ. But it is also the beginning of the church's reflection upon and interpretation of its faith—what we call tradition.

Clearly one of the most important arguments that can be used against any changes in our way of naming and speaking about God is that from tradition. In addition, many Roman Catholics, Orthodox, and some Anglicans who oppose the ordination of women argue that, while the teaching of Scripture itself may not be altogether conclusive on this issue, the consistent tradition of the church has been that only men may be ordained to the priesthood. But the notion of tradition, when used this way, is very unclear. Does it mean simply that the *custom* of the church has not been to ordain women, or does it intend to convey a greater authority?

We can see a similar confusion between tradition and custom in the New Testament itself. When Gentiles began to seek baptism in the Christian community, the Jewish followers of Jesus found it necessary to change some of the traditions they had known. In his letter to the Galatians, for example, Paul argued against circumcision of the new converts, and would not require them to submit to the whole Law, which required males to be circumcised. There were, he argued, other more compelling considerations, namely, the freedom we have through faith in Christ Jesus. Similarly, Peter, we are told in Acts 10, abandoned the prohibition against the eating of certain foods because they were (by tradition or custom) unclean. Jesus himself often cast to one side, or radically changed, the traditions of the elders, frequently saying, "It was said to you of old time, but I say to you...." The traditions of Judaism passed down in the Law were important, giving the people a sense of identity with one another and with God, but they were not beyond change. They could be treated as customs; that is, they could be modified or abandoned altogether if other circumstances made them no longer appropriate.

Many clergy today have endured a similar confusion between custom and tradition in their parishes, although the confusion may be somewhat less serious. A new priest or minister is often told by a member of the congregation: "our tradition here is...." The "tradition" can range from how the sanctuary is decorated at Christmas to which translation of the Bible has been used for the past several years. When used in such a way, the "tradition" usually means how certain people remember the way things have "always" been done, or how the previous pastor did things.

A similar attitude pervades many political campaigns. Especially when running for office, politicians like to talk about a return to "traditional values," particularly in the area of sexual morality. Talk of "traditional values" usually means that we should return to what we like to think were the values in the "golden age" of our own past. Most of the time, of course, that "golden age," when everyone was pure and virtuous, never existed. Yet it is how we like to think the past was, and so we call it the "tradition." Someone once remarked that the person who does not know history is condemned to live only in a fairly recent past.

This confusion between custom and tradition can at times be more irritating or amusing than serious; at other times it can have serious theological consequences. For example, Paul was persecuted, he says in Galatians, because he denied the necessity of circumcision. And Jesus was crucified because he went against the customs of the elders: namely, he called God *Abba*, he overthrew the tables of the money changers in the Temple, he healed on the Sabbath, and he claimed to forgive sinners. In our own day many women in the Roman Catholic Church believe their calling to the ordained ministry is frustrated by the appeal to the "tradition" that only men can be ordained. Moreover, many women and men in all of the churches believe themselves excluded by the "traditional" use of exclusively masculine names for God. Obviously the notion of tradition must be more carefully analyzed and clarified.

Tradition, in what might be called the legitimate theological and liturgical sense, refers to doctrine and liturgical practices as they have developed in the church's life, starting with the New Testament. The New Testament itself is the beginning of the church's tradition because it is the written record of the several traditions concerning Jesus—stories told about him, recollections of his teaching, his appearances after the crucifixion, and so forth. Paul in 1 Corinthians 11 speaks of the "tradition" handed down to him concerning the Last Supper, some years before these stories were recorded in the gospels. But in the same chapter he speaks of the "tradition" of veiling a woman's head when she prays, and he derides as unnatural men who have long hair—traditions that we today would regard as mere customs, certainly not to be compared with the tradition of the eucharist. Customs associated with the eucharist—what it means, how it is to be offered, and how often it is offered—have changed over the centuries, but the eucharist itself has remained at the center of the church's tradition. In a similar way the Apostles' Creed as we know it today developed out of the tradition of requiring converts to confess their faith at baptism.[13] In other words, tradition is the process through which the Christian community in a particular time and place interprets and adapts to its own situation what it has received in the gospel of salvation.

The true preaching of the faith always calls for a new assimilation and translation of the traditional faith, as well as loyalty to revelation and its historical transmission. Such a "translation," if only because it must start from the experience of a given age and speak the language of the times, will perhaps use new terms to formulate the Catholic faith, while still dealing with a dogma that remains the same. Words change their meaning in the course of history.[14]

So the tradition of the church is not something cut and dried, a given body of received knowledge. On the contrary, tradition is the living and vital response of the community to the leading of the Spirit while seeking to remain faithful to what has been revealed. At times those new expressions of the faith of the community can be less than faithful to the truth of the Gospel; at other times, new ways of thinking and believing may enable us to hear its saving word more clearly or deeply. Which of those possibilities is the more likely is the issue involved in our present controversies about language and names.

The church's tradition expresses the ongoing history of the people of God—where we have come from, where we are now, and where we may be called in the future. In this sense, nebulous as it may seem, tradition is authoritative; it deepens and enhances faith in Christ's Gospel through its interpretation of Scripture and the apostolic faith.

In the first chapter we looked at the two central names for God in Scripture—I Am and Father—and we have seen some of the problems people today have with both. What I have hoped to show through this discussion of authority is that the language we use about God, especially the names we use for God, needs always to be open to the continuing experience of Christian people as God meets them. Certainly this does not mean we can abandon the great revealed names for God; they must always serve as a continuing source for revealing the nature of God to us. But it does mean that names can change their meaning and are open to reinterpretation.

Similarly, we must be open to the possibility of new ways of speaking about God—whether to correct or balance the strong dominance of one set of images, or to express the reality of God in different cultures. The authority of new ways of speaking about God will be found in the degree to which they can provide us with a deeper vision of God and a deeper hearing of God's Word spoken to us.

All names, whether of God or anything else, are interpretations of a reality that is ultimately hidden from us, and they all fall short of the reality they would name. For that reason they are sacramental; they direct us to the reality, but are not to be confused with it. In other words, they are outward and visible signs of the mystery towards which they direct us. Here, where we live as creatures in space and time, we are not yet one with God. For that reason the names are vital, if only to remind us, whenever we use them, that they are not the reality itself; they can only direct us to the God who utterly transcends us, but who is also present with us.

CHAPTER III

Praying the Mystery

▪ 1 ▪

S cripture and tradition are very important, but they are not enough for the Christian life. They talk about God and God's revelation to us in an authoritative way, but we need more than statements and propositions to believe in God. It is like the difference between saying, "I believe *that* Mary is a good woman" and "I believe *in* Mary." For me to believe in a person commits me to much more than a simple statement of belief about something. It commits me to a relationship.

I cannot make a statement like "I believe in Mary" on short acquaintance. Even though we may speak of falling in love at "first sight," we know it rarely happens. To love someone enough to be able to say "I believe in you" requires a long period of getting to know that person. Believing in someone calls for, and arises out of, love and trust. In our ordinary human relationships, as we know, the kind of love and trust that enables us to believe in someone involves, among other things, conversation, time spent together, the sharing of pains and joys, as well as all the trivial things that happen during the course of a day. When we know someone well, well enough to be able to say "I believe in you," then we can use that person's name with much greater authority. That name will call up and express the history we have had together, and what our hopes may be for the future.

So it is with God. When we say in the creeds of the church, "We believe in God," as in the creed of Nicea, or "I believe in God," as in the baptismal creed, we are expressing a relationship with one whom we have to some degree got to know, love, and trust. Obviously such affirmations of belief in God do not always carry the same weight of conviction. In the seminary where I teach, we go to chapel frequently, and I often have found myself early in the morning mumbling "I believe in God" without much conviction. But when I stop to think about what I am doing, I know that I am expressing my belief in one who knows me better than I know myself, and one whom I hope I shall someday come to know more deeply and completely than I have ever known anyone.

The journey of coming to love, trust, and believe in God is the journey of prayer. Without the life of prayer all of our language about God would be meaningless; it would be idle chatter about someone whom we do not know. All that we have to say about God finds its meaning and justification in the relationship we have with the God whom, we believe, we can call by name and who, we believe, hears us. There is much truth in the ancient saying, "A theologian is a person who prays, and a person who prays is a theologian."[1]

Prayer, then, is our living in the mystery of God and having a personal relationship with that mystery. It enables us to do more than simply speak about it. Indeed, one of the reasons why naming God is so crucial for many people at the present time is that we believe in a God who is not an abstract principle, but who is personal, who is at the deepest center of our existence as persons, who is utterly transcendent and without a name, yet also Emmanuel, God with us. It is in prayer that we enter into personal relationship with such a God. And as with all personal relationships, the names we use in order to pray to God need to express our history with God and our hopes for the future.

How we are to name God in our prayers, then, is of great importance, just as our naming of other people is important. In both cases those names will carry with them the authority of a personal relationship. That authority is not, of course, greater than the authority of Scripture and tradition, and our way of naming God out of our prayer must be shaped by these norms. Still, the names we give to God out of our life of prayer have an authority that is closer to home, closer to the center out of which we pray.

Praying is one of those activities which can be absolutely simple and terribly complex, both at the same time. It is simple when you actually do it, but complex when you stop to think about it—somewhat like riding a bicycle or driving a car. It would seem to arise quite naturally out of the human spirit, out of our turning to something beyond ourselves in supplication, or wonder, or thanksgiving. And yet it seems an odd thing to do—turning to some heavenly being for something which I ought to be able to do on my own, or projecting onto the heavens my childish relationship with the parents who always "took care of me."[2] Prayer is an intensely personal activity—one should be as cautious about sharing the contents of one's prayers as about sharing one's dreams. And yet there are times when people come together as a community in order to pray, times when it seems absolutely right and neces-sary to share our need or our thanksgiving with others, whether in small groups or formal services of worship. Even in a society as secular as our own, im-portant events, such as the inauguration of a president or a natural disaster, always seem to call for prayer. We can be cynical about that, but it does seem to re-flect a desire to offer what is happening to "a higher power," a sense that we cannot do it all on our own.

This book is not a treatise on prayer, but it is con-cerned with the relationship between our praying and our naming of God. Consequently, a few things must be said about prayer if we are to see how they are re-lated to one another. Prayer includes both what I do when I am alone with God and what I do when I wor-ship with others; it is both personal and corporate, not individualistic or solitary. I do not pray all by myself, but, as the ancient liturgy puts it, I join my voice "with angels and archangels and with all the company of heaven," as well as with all the people who are also offering their prayers.

I once had a parishioner who was very faithful in at-tending weekday services, where there were only one or two people present, but she never attended the principal service on Sunday morning. When I asked her at a dinner party why this was so, she said, "I don't like dealing with all those people. I like to be alone with God." The occasion was not the best one for making a theological response, but it does need to be made here—prayer is never solitary, never something we do all on our own. How we understand the personal and corporate nature of prayer has significant con-sequences for our naming of God.

First, a few theological generalities about the structure of Christian prayer might be helpful. Whether personal or corporate, prayer arises out of what we believe about God, in particular what is shown to us about God in Jesus Christ and in the presence of the Holy Spirit in our lives. Most liturgical prayers end with the phrase "through Jesus Christ our Lord, who lives and reigns with you and the Holy Spirit, one God, now and forever." In other words, central to Christian prayer is our belief in the God who reaches out to us and who communicates with us in Word and Spirit— God as trinity of persons, as Christians have confessed since the earliest days of the church.

Now some of the language used to name the persons of the Trinity in the traditional formulations—Father, Son, and Holy Spirit—has become problematical for those who object to the predominately masculine imagery. Even the doctrine itself has become problematical for those who argue that trinitarian doctrine is unnecessary and mystifying.[3] One leading feminist theologian, Patricia Wilson-Kastner, however, has argued forcefully for the doctrine, which she believes is vital for a feminist perspective on God with its theology of divine relationships. She believes we cannot precipitously abandon language that is so rooted in Scripture and in the liturgical tradition:

> To discard completely the Father-Son terminology of trinitarian language would present serious difficulties, because one could easily lose sight of the interpersonal aspects of the relationship. Intrinsically, Mother-Daughter images can be equally useful; ways could also be found to introduce and explore this expression of relationship. Terms such as "creator, redeemer, and sanctifier" can be helpful, but indicate only the relationship of God to us, rather than the inner life of the trinitarian God in whom we are invited

to participate. The new formula may be a useful addition to liturgical and theological language, but it cannot be a substitute for the older formula.[4]

I do not believe we can allow the controversies now surrounding the names Father and Son to prevent us from exploring the trinitarian nature of prayer. Those controversies can only be resolved with much patience and attentive listening by those on both sides of the issue. In what I have to say here I shall try to be as sensitive as possible to the problem, while not abandoning the names Father and Son which have come to us in the tradition.

The reason why the trinitarian nature of God is central to our understanding of prayer, as Wilson-Kastner has pointed out, is that it directs us to the relationship we have with God—which is one of the sources for our naming God. In Jesus Christ, Christians believe, God reaches out to us, and in the Holy Spirit dwells in us. The church struggled long and hard in the first centuries of its existence to define and clarify what it meant by such beliefs. Two dimensions of that struggle are important for us here. First, in the Incarnation the Word became a human being, a man, taking the form of a servant in order to share in our humanity and to make it God's own. Jesus Christ is, as the ancient formulas put it, "true God and true man." And God did this in order that we might enter into a relationship which is personal.

In other words, our relationship with God is not through a book, nor through oracles, nor through some abstraction; it is the fulfillment of what we know now imperfectly in personal relationships, such as

marriage, friendship, parenthood—all those relationships in which we become more ourselves by sharing
our lives with others. That is what the Incarnation is
all about: God's life, Being, is shared with us in Jesus
Christ.

Second, God remains with us in the Holy Spirit, the
gift of God's own self. Gifts can be of many kinds, and
through them we seek to express love, affection, and
concern. We can even give our life for another in order
that someone else may live. The Holy Spirit is the gift
of God—not merely *to* us, as we would give a gift to
another, but *in* us, in the "heart," as Scripture puts it.
It is a gift that makes us able to respond to God with
our selves in prayer, witness, and service. In other
words, the triune nature of God makes it possible for
us to believe that in the Holy Spirit God is praying in
us, teaching us, as St. Paul says, how to pray (Rom. 8:
26). By the Spirit of God, we are made able to pray to
God in, through, and with Jesus Christ, who is one
with us and one with God.

Christians do not pray across a great gulf to a God ✓
who is far off. Rather we pray with a God who has become one with us in Jesus Christ and whose Spirit
dwells in us. To pray through Jesus Christ and with
him is to believe that our lives, along with the lives of
all human beings in their complexity and sin, are held
up and offered in Christ to the creator of all that is.
And it is the Spirit of God that makes such prayer
possible. To pray through Jesus Christ means that the
humanity of every woman and man is, in hope, united
to the eternal Word and Son, and is offered to the
Father through the offering of the great High Priest,
who has taken our humanity for his own.

I have learned over the years that the most difficult and even frightening aspect of prayer, whether personal or corporate, is that I have to be honest with myself. When I am talking to other people, I can use language to conceal as well as to reveal myself; I can hide behind words.[5] But when I pray through Jesus Christ in the Spirit of God, I must meet myself, and I must try to see myself as God sees me. Otherwise I am only praying to the idol that I create for myself. I can only pray as the complex person I am—with all my weaknesses and strengths, my desires and hopes, my fears and anxieties. "It is a fearful thing to fall into the hands of the living God" (Heb. 10:31), because in prayer to the living God I must confront myself. In my prayer I also bring with me my personal history, much of which I would rather forget.

I also have to bring my culture—the fact that I am a white, male, middle-class American, and a reasonably successful professional. I am also a sexual person; my sexuality and how I express it are also factors in my praying. When I am sexually attracted to another person, I pray for that person differently than I might pray for someone else. All of that forms and shapes my prayer, as indeed does the fact that I have learned to pray in the very formal tradition of the Book of Common Prayer of the Episcopal Church, and through the ordered reading of Holy Scripture. If I were female or black or working class, if I were poor or critically ill, my prayers would reflect that identity and condition. If I were married, I could not pray without the constant awareness in my prayers of my spouse.

All of this points to the work of the Spirit in me as I seek to pray, as myself, in the humanity of Christ. Because Christ has taken my humanity to himself, *I* am present to God—just as I am, not as some idealized version of myself. To be present to God in prayer requires a courage and an honesty I cannot have on my own—the Spirit prays in me, giving me the courage to pray.[6]

There is, however, a deeper dimension to prayer through Jesus Christ in the Holy Spirit, one which is of even greater importance when we think of the names of God we use in corporate worship. Prayer through Jesus Christ in the Spirit involves more than just an individual praying alone. When Christian people gather to pray together, they become more than just a collection of individuals who happen to be doing the same thing. They become a community, a body, gathered together for common prayer.

Or at least that is what ought to be the case. More often, like my former parishioner, we tend to think of ourselves as being "alone with God." The reasons for this are, of course, many. We live in a highly individualistic society in which many people believe they have to make it on their own. As has become increasingly evident in the business world, the sense that one has a responsibility to others, whether to fellow-workers or customers, seems to have been lost in the midst of corporate mergers, take-overs, and the like. Families tend to turn in on themselves in suburban developments, while those who live alone are isolated in large apartment complexes. It is inevitable that when such people gather to pray on Sunday morning, they will not easily become a community, but will continue to think of themselves as isolated from the person in the next pew, and even more isolated from the people outside the church building.

One of the things I have learned after many years of teaching in an Episcopal seminary, however, is that the majority of our students come to seminary because they are seeking a community, a place where they can discover themselves as they pray and worship with others, even with those they may not like or with whom they have serious disagreements. In such a community of corporate prayer, I am enabled to encounter others. Thus, when I pray for people in Albania who have been killed in an earthquake, or for the starving in Ethiopia, or for all the sick and suffering in my own town—people whose names I do not even know—I overcome some of my sense of separateness.

Christians are called to be a community at prayer, and this fact has many important consequences, not least for the way in which we address God by name. Because we believe that in Jesus Christ God is united with our humanity—that is, the humanity of every single person, not just Christians and not just the people we know—we must also believe that we are in Christ united to every single human being. The person killed in Albania, or the person dying in the next apartment, is my brother or sister. This belief is hard to express in words and it is even harder to act upon, but it is what we are called to as Christians. Many people who see another person in a desperate condition have been known to say, "There but for the grace of God go I," but what the Christian really ought to say is, "There by the grace of God go I; this is someone united to me in Jesus Christ."

Our prayer offers with it the prayer, articulate or inarticulate, spoken or only a cry of hope, of every human being. We all share in the humanity of Christ. The pain and suffering, the joy, hope, and desires of every person are present to God through our praying in Christ, just as all that I am is present to God through the prayers of others, however they may be offered and in whatever name they may be said. Because we pray in, through, and with Christ, we are not merely praying for others, we are praying with them. The prayer of the woman in Africa who prays for her starving child or the prayer of the man in Latin America who prays for his release from a prison—both are one with my prayers for and with a friend dying of AIDS.

▪ 2 ▪

The names we use to address God in prayer arise out of the ways all human beings name themselves, how they say who they are, and what they hope for themselves. When I was first ordained and was being introduced to the parish where I was to serve, the senior warden, who had known me as a child, introduced me to the congregation as "the Reverend Jimmy Griffiss." Because of my new pride in being a priest I was quite offended, since I certainly did not think of myself—before God or before the congregation—as "Jimmy," but as James or Fr. Griffiss. In other words my name, I believed, should reflect my new status, and I wanted God to think of me that way when I prayed. As the years have gone by, and (I hope) some of my arrogance has left me, I realize that I can quite easily be "Jimmy" in the presence of God—although not yet in the presence of a congregation!

The point of this autobiographical anecdote is important. I come before God in prayer with an identity of my own and that identity affects how I pray, because who I am is expressed in the name I give myself. "Jimmy" suggests a child, dependent upon others, and it speaks of affection and closeness. "James," on the other hand, suggests an adult, someone to be treated with respect, perhaps even with distance.

In other words, how I name myself will affect the way I name God. At times my prayer may be that of a child, speaking to a father or mother in whose care I know I am held. At other times I may think of myself as a responsible and independent person, meeting God, so to speak, as a friend or equal. Although I know theologically that I can never be an equal with God, nonetheless it can be a relationship which is more aptly expressed by such names as Lord or the Holy One, or as Being Itself, the One Who Is, because I do not use names of parenting, the names that derive from my childhood.

All the names we use to address God point to a reality that can never be totally exhausted by our naming, but that is conveyed to us in the naming. We know the truth of this when we think of naming another person, especially one with whom we are very close. We know that no name we can use for another person or for our relationship with that person can ever fully and completely identify who that person is, what he or she may become in the future, and how the nature of the relationship itself may change as each of us grows or fails to grow. To say that another person is a wife or husband, a lover or friend, even an enemy, is to touch upon a reality that is largely hidden from us even though we are living in the relationship itself. All pastors, especially those who have been involved in counseling married people, know the sad histories that lead to divorce or separation—histories that often begin with the phrase, "He is not the person I thought I was marrying ten years ago," or "She has not grown with me; she can no longer be a companion for me; all she thinks of is the children." Friends, who are not bound by marriage vows, often have the same experience. A person who was my best friend at the age of twenty may well move in totally different directions as he or she develops an individuality and personality through age and experience, so that when we meet twenty years later there is very little for us to talk about.

On the other hand, of course, we have all known those relationships where two human beings do grow together for forty or fifty years, and in which a name conveys all that they have shared during those years. But even then, as all married people and friends know, there still remains in the relationship a dimension that cannot be fully known and named. It is what we call the inner being of a person, his or her identity as a self with its own hiddenness and privacy—a self which, as St. Paul suggests, is known only to God, or, as the Psalmist says, only God knows the innermost secrets of the heart.

Our naming of ourselves and our naming of others is similar to our naming God in prayer and worship. While most of the time, at least, we believe that God's love and care are steadfast, we also know we are changing as we grow in our relationship with God. Our names for God will inevitably reflect the changes that are taking place within ourselves. When I was a child I prayed as a child would pray to some father or mother figure in the heavens who had the power to give—or withhold—everything I asked for. But as an adult, as one who must to a very considerable degree make his own way in the world, I can no longer pray that way; I may no longer be able to name God in ways that express a child's image of God. As an adult I know times when my prayer to God is empty and meaningless, when I am simply repeating words and when the names I use—Father, Almighty, Savior, and so forth— mean very little. They are names I may repeat by rote, not names that convey the deep longings of my heart at a time when God's love and care seem far from me.

Still, there are times now when I can address God as Mother or Father and be reminded of the depth of a personal relationship of care and concern. There are also times when I can name God as Almighty, Savior, Sanctifier, and know what I mean by those names because I know the steadfastness of God's love and care in my life. I believe such an experience is familiar to all Christians, and to all people who reflect upon their relationships, whether it be a relationship with God or with another human being, or even with themselves. Some of the names we use in these relationships, as well as the names with which we identify ourselves, speak to us at one time more powerfully than at another. As I said earlier, there are times when the nickname "Jimmy" identifies me, while at other times "James" identifies me more clearly to myself and others. Or there are times when I can call another per-

son "my friend" with deep significance, but there may
be other times when that name will be less meaningful. It is not that the names themselves have ceased to
be significant, but that we know and understand ourselves and others differently.

Such is also the case with the names we use to
speak to God. There are times when I would not want
to speak to God as Father or Mother, because I want to
express something else of importance in my relationship with God and in my understanding of myself. For
example, sometimes I can speak to God much more
readily as a friend or companion, one who loves me not
as a parent loves a child, but as one who chooses me as
a friend. To use one name for God in prayer is not to
deny the legitimacy of other names. Rather, it is to recognize that my naming of God reflects my own understanding of myself at a particular time, as a person
who is changing and growing in relationship with God.
In addition, it is to recognize that the people with
whom I pray are themselves changing and growing in
their relationship with God.

In today's world many women and some men are
beginning to recognize that they cannot easily pray to
God as Father. In spite of the meaning of the name
"Father" in the biblical and liturgical traditions, the
name still carries with it the sense of masculine control and dominance—an understanding by no means
limited to women, since men can be abused or
oppressed or neglected by their fathers. In the same
way many women and men have had painful relationships with their mothers, which makes that image of
God equally difficult for them. When I am really aware
that I am praying with other people, offering my pray-

ers with them, and not just praying out of my own solitude, then I must also be aware that there are those for whom the names Father or Mother do not convey the care that parents ideally take for their children. I may want to use such names in my own prayers, but I have to recognize and accept that those names may present serious difficulties for others with whom I am praying. The woman or man who was sexually or physically abused by a father or mother may need to find other names with which to speak to God in prayer.

We western Christians, who live in democratic societies, must also recognize that many of the names from the biblical and liturgical tradition may themselves convey offensive images of the God to whom others wish to pray. In many parts of Latin America or Spain, names like Lord or Señor carry overtones of the oppressor: the man or woman who owns all of the land in a particular location, and who controls the life of the peasants who own no land.

The language of oppression and domination is also frequent in the Old Testament. The Psalter pictures a God who leads the people into battle, who seeks the destruction of their enemies, and who encourages them to eliminate those who, like the Canaanites, resist the chosen people of Yahweh.[7] Such a warlike image of God is not popular today, and so what we need when reading the Psalter or when listening to lessons from the Old Testament is more interpretation. We need to put these ideas in context and go beyond their blatant surface meanings to make them better able to express what we believe about God. Do we really believe in a God of vengeance, as these names might imply? Just as some people may have difficulty in praying to a God who is named Father or Mother, so too many Christians may have difficulty in praying to a God who is described in military terms.

Too often Christians have identified their political and imperialistic aspirations with God's cause. In fairly recent times, for example, many Americans have seen Soviet Russia as an enemy of God and encouraged the idea that God should lead us in a holy crusade against that nation. There have been many other times in Christian history when our names have conveyed images of God that would cause us much difficulty today. The concern of women about overt masculine imagery is only a continuation of a long-standing problem we Christians have: how to interpret the ancient names in terms of our modern sensibilities. We do not think of God—unless we are militantly anti-communist—as a warrior who is on our side against another nation. Nor in a similar way can many women and men think of God as a Father or a Lord, when those names convey an image that is no longer acceptable to them.

Somehow what we all must do, both in our private prayer and in our common worship, is find a way we can share the same God with others. This is the hard work of prayer; the names that I use may not speak with sufficient power to enable others to enter into the mystery of God. In other words I must name God, even to myself, in such a way that the names I use enable me to offer others to God, for that is what prayer is—an offering with others to the mystery of all things, one who cannot be limited by any name.

How do we do that? I believe the answer to that question lies in our doctrine of God. It must be a theological answer and not simply a sentimental one, an answer that simply appeals to whatever feelings people have about God. As I shall show in the next chapter, there is a legitimate sense in which the experience that people have of God can be—and indeed must be—a valid source for their naming of God. But praying the names of God must also arise out of what we believe about the God to whom we pray.

To be a Christian is to believe that Jesus Christ is the presence of God in our history and has taken our humanity into God. Along with other human beings, we pray through the names that have arisen in our common humanity, even those names for which we can claim the authority of revelation in Holy Scripture. All of the names human beings use for God only direct us to the mystery; they are concrete expressions of what we believe to be true about God, signs to us of a transcendent reality. But at the same time they cannot be confused with the reality itself, nor can they restrict the reality of God. God transcends every sign, just as God transcends every name.

To use an example which is familiar to most Christians, we believe that in the sacramental life of the church there are two fundamental signs, baptism and eucharist, that define how we related to God in Christ. Those two sacramental signs do not restrict the presence of God in our history; there are many others signs of God's presence with us. But those two fundamental signs structure how we believe God is with us in many other ways. They express how we believe God continues to be present with us, how the transcendent one is present with us concretely. The historically concrete, the particular instance, this bread and wine, this water, this particular man, Jesus of Nazareth—all are absolutely necessary for the Christian understanding of how God is present. Without them we would be lost in a nebulous cloud of spiritualism that has no relationship with concrete historical presence. And yet these signs do not define, limit, or exhaust the reality of the transcendent God. They show us God, but they show us a God who is still hidden from our eyes and mind.

So too do the names that we use for God. We must use names because we are speaking about a God who is personal, not an "it." We speak to God as Father, Mother, Friend, Lover, because we are speaking to one who is closer to us than we are to ourselves, one who has in Jesus become one with us. Yet we also know that our speaking to God is not like speaking to a father, mother, lover, or friend, because we are speaking to one who utterly transcends all of those descriptions.

CHAPTER IV

Experiencing God

▪ 1 ▪

In previous chapters I have examined three areas that are fundamental both to our naming of God and to our use of any kind of language at all about God. First, I explored to some degree the biblical language about God, especially the two most important names for God in Scripture: "I Am" or Yahweh, the most holy name for God in the Old Testament and the one that is central to Israel's understanding of its relationship to God, and "Father," which is central to the preaching of Jesus and to the theology of Paul and other New Testament writers. Since many Christians would consider both names to carry with them the authority of biblical revelation,[1] I then looked at how we might understand the authority of Scripture and tradition in order to see how such names can be authoritative for us.

Finally, I discussed the kind of language that arises out of our prayer and worship, that is, out of our encounter with God in what we call our spiritual lives, that inmost center the Bible calls our "heart." The language of prayer and worship is close to us, because it arises out of the desire of our hearts for God. Even though Scripture and the worshiping tradition of the church structure our belief in God as one who reaches out to us in Christ and the Spirit, nonetheless, the hearts of most human beings, no matter what their religious tradition, would seem to be restless until they can find rest in God. There is a long and important tradition in Christian thinking about the spiritual life that recognizes that human beings do seek for God as their center, even when they have not been able to identify God by a name that is recognizable to Christians.[2]

Because our life of prayer and worship is so central and important to us, it presents the most difficulties both for those who object to changes in our customary language about God and those who are calling for these changes. However, as I suggested in the last chapter, new ways of talking about God may well arise as Christian people encounter God in prayer. We must remember, after all, that much of the Christian language about God has itself been an innovation. To address God in the trinitarian form as Father, Son, and Holy Spirit, or to speak of Jesus as Savior and Lord, for example, is unknown in Judaism. As we have seen in an earlier chapter, the use of such language involved much debate and even polemical attacks in the early church. Christians defended the use of such language because it arose out of their life of prayer and worship. So too, perhaps, shall we have to develop language about God that arises out of similar experience.

In this chapter I want to explore more deeply what we mean when we talk about experiencing God, and how that can affect our way of naming God. But to talk about "experiencing God" is itself difficult, because the concept of "experience" is so complex. In theology and philosophy, it has a variety of meanings; in ordinary speech, its meaning can be even more obscure. It can range from the vague and sentimental use—such as "I had a *marvelous* experience yesterday"—to the profoundly serious—"I have had a conversion experience." As I shall discuss later, we must use the word very carefully, especially when we are concerned with its importance for the ways in which we might name God. It will not do to talk about "experiencing God" in a way that could be construed as sentimental and innocuous; the human experience of God is more mysterious and fundamental than that!

So in order to use the word carefully some historical and philosophical discussion is necessary. Concepts like "experience" have histories, and without an understanding of this history we can easily misuse them. I believe it is necessary, then, to look first at some of the developments that have taken place in western Christianity, and to see how those developments have resulted in new ways of understanding ourselves, our experience, and our world, and hence in new ways of naming God.

Beginning with the period of the Renaissance and Reformation, certain shifts began to take place in the way human beings in Europe and later in the United States understood themselves, their relationship with the world around them, and their relationship with God. The way we understand our relationship with God reflects how we understand ourselves and our world; such an understanding does not occur in a vacuum, but reflects who we are. If I am the kind of person who is used to getting his own way because of my money, connections, or personal charm, I shall in all likelihood understand my relationship with God differently than if I am poor, oppressed, and without any resources whatsoever. On the one hand, I shall assume God is "on my side" as I go through life; on the other, I shall probably think of God—or at least of the churches that represent God—as the oppressor, as one who is punishing me because of my sins or failures.

The New Testament provides an illuminating parallel. People who were dispossessed of their land—those who were called "sinners" because they could not live according to the Law—no doubt understood God quite differently than did the wealthy Pharisees, who could fulfill the Law and think of themselves as righteous before God. The gospels suggest quite frequently that the "sinners" responded to the preaching of Jesus much more readily than did the Pharisees, who saw Jesus as an antagonist. How the Word of God is heard, whether in New Testament times or now, reflects the condition of those who hear it.

To take another example, when St. Anselm attempted to explain how Jesus saves us from our sins, he chose as an analogy the feudal structure of the society in which he lived—and compared the Atonement to making satisfaction to a feudal overlord. A theologian today, however, would in all probability find such an image unsatisfactory, since we do not—or ought not!—think of God in such terms. I often say to my students that theologians and philosophers, like preachers, do not sit around making up new doctrines, concepts, or sermon illustrations. They simply reflect their time and condition in life.[3]

In the period of the Renaissance and Reformation, so crucial for the development of what we call "modern consciousness," there were several significant shifts in how human beings understood themselves and their world. There was, first of all, an increased awareness of historical development and change, as historians, biblical scholars, and theologians began to study the past and to examine how it was different from the present. The idea that the context within which someone thought, or wrote, or painted needed to be taken into account in understanding ideas or images, was quite new. We are all familiar, for example, with paintings that show biblical figures in the dress and surroundings of medieval Europe. The artist saw no need for setting a biblical story in its own time and place, nor did he seek historical verisimilitude—biblical figures could have blonde hair and Saxon features. A theologian such as Thomas Aquinas in the thirteenth century could say, when criticized for using ancient and pagan philosophers in his theology, that it did not matter when these people lived and wrote; all that mattered was whether what they said was true. Truth itself had an existence quite removed from its historical context. Today we study the philosophers Plato and Aristotle as historical figures; for Aquinas, they were contemporaries.

Such an attitude began to change in the sixteenth century, however, when it came to be recognized that the time in which people lived and wrote had consequences for what they said or did, and that "truth" itself might change and develop. The way in which people experienced their world and understood it, in other words, was not always the same; their ideas and images could be filtered through new and contemporary lenses. Two areas of change are immediately obvious: the development of historical scholarship in the study of Scripture and doctrine, and the use of a scientific and empirical methodology in the study of the natural order. Erasmus initiated the critical study of the text of the New Testament; other scholars questioned the papal claims for temporal jurisdiction in western Europe (the so-called Donation of Constantine); and Luther and other reformers denounced indulgences, the sacrifice of the Mass, Purgatory, and many other doctrines that had been thought to come directly from the apostles themselves. Old beliefs, hallowed by tradition, were called into question and often abandoned. This trend continued into the nineteenth century as Scripture and tradition more and more became the subject of historical investigation and questioning. Over the course of several centuries, people came to see that both biblical writers and theologians were conditioned by the time in which they lived, and that the beliefs that they had inherited as part of a supposedly unchanging tradition may themselves have been culture-bound.[4]

It was in the area of what we now call science that some of the most dramatic changes took place. What theologians had to say about the Bible might be important to some people, but what scientists had to say about the world in which people actually lived affected their lives more directly and immediately. As natural philosophers (as they were then called) began to look more critically at the world around them, they began to demonstrate that the fixed and unchanging world as pictured in the Bible was an illusion. Galileo and Copernicus proposed the theory that the earth was not the center of the universe, and that in fact it moved around the sun. One assertion after another by scientists during the next several centuries called into question the authority of Scripture. Human beings began to think of themselves no longer as the center of a divinely created and stable universe, but as a miniscule part of a vastly expanding and evolving universe. Much to the consternation of the theologians of his time, Darwin even argued that the human species itself was descended from lower forms of animal life.

If we think today that some of the movements in the church are too radical and "unbiblical"—inclusive language, the ordination of women, the questioning of customary sexual morality, and the like—we would do well to remember the past. Galileo and Darwin radically shook the foundations of biblical authority, especially the validity of the creation story in Genesis. Most of what they argued is now commonly accepted by us in the twentieth century, but such ideas were very radical in their time. Consequently the way we see the world is not the same as people saw it in the thirteenth century, nor in the time of Jesus himself. Theologians and preachers can no longer pretend that it is, unless, of course, they want to forget the historical and scientific context in which they proclaim the Gospel. We now need to *interpret* much of what Holy Scripture says to us simply because we are beings who recognize and accept historical change in our concepts and images.

Although historical consciousness and a scientific, empirical methodology are of central importance in the development of modern consciousness, there is another area that, I believe, is of still greater significance, especially for the concerns with which I am dealing in this book. It is the increased awareness of personal subjectivity, both in our relationship to the world and in our relationship to God. By "personal subjectivity" I mean our awareness of the role of our personal history in our understanding of anything whatsoever—God, family, friends, and so forth. We live—for better or worse—in an "I"-centered world, one in which the controlling factor is how I understand myself in my relationships with others. Some preachers and theologians might want to condemn such egocentricity simply as another example of modern sinfulness and our abandonment of God and the Bible—the "ME generation," as it is called. But to do so is superficial. Personal subjectivity is not just a consequence of human pride and concupiscence—something that has always been with us. It represents another way of understanding the world and ourselves, one in which personal and individual identity is of greater importance than the communal and corporate.

We can see the beginning of such an understanding in western thinking as early as St. Augustine, the father of much western theology. In his *Confessions* Augustine wrote about the personal turmoil in his relationship with God, his awareness of his sin, and of the grounding of his Christian faith in his personal identity. Similarly Martin Luther's experience of salvation was more grounded in who he was as a person, his sense of self, than in the teachings of the church. He came to know his justification out of the depths of his own personal turmoil.[5] This sense of interiority, of personal subjectivity, is one of the things that has made Augustine and Luther so attractive to us in the present century. Unlike so many other theologians, who can be very abstract, they seem to speak to the heart and not only to the intellect. They seem to speak from "experience."

These two figures stand in contrast to much of classical theology, which developed prior to the Renaissance. It assumed a philosophical world view in which the revelations of Scripture or the knowledge gained through experience were thought to be objectively true; that the Genesis account of creation was the way it actually happened, for example, or that evidence of our senses accurately reflects the world. As we might say nowadays, it assumed that facts are facts. These facts did not depend upon the point of view of the knower, whose knowledge was limited only by ignorance, not by any deeply held, perhaps even unconscious, assumptions about the world.

However, as human beings continued to reflect upon the knowledge that was given to them through revelation and through sense experience, the matter was seen to be more complex. As the study of history and of the natural order grew, while the authority of biblical revelation was increasingly called into question, it began to be recognized that knowledge from any source involves a total attitude towards the world in which we live. Our knowledge is never simply objective, but colored by the prejudices and assumptions of human beings.

To establish the facts in a court of law, for example, requires more than one witness. Facts are not always clear and unambiguous. Or, to put the matter more simply, if we don't believe something ought to be so, then we may not see it, or if we do, our perceptions may conform to what we believe ought to be the case. If we really believe that "nice people" don't do certain things, for instance, then we can usually avoid accepting the fact that they do them. How often have we heard it said, or even said it ourselves, that a minister of the Gospel would not cheat, or lie, or commit any act of sexual immorality, thus completely ignoring the facts of life?

Many times the way in which our personal prejudices get in the way of our knowledge of the "facts" is trivial and can be easily corrected. But there are times when it is much more serious. Factual data are not simply hard bits of information that stand in isolation from other things we know or believe; they are not as "factual" or "objective" as we might like to think. In our interpretation of historical data, for example, we often filter out those "facts" that do not fit into our presuppositions about how events have taken place. For many centuries, for example, it was assumed that women had made no contribution to the development of western theology. Even the presence of such major theological figures as Teresa of Avila and Julian of Norwich did not challenge the assumption that only men did theology.[6] Women, it was thought, did not have the intellectual capacity to be theologians and philosophers, so their contributions became invisible, either ignored or dismissed by the predominately male theological community. The feminist movement, however, has clearly shown that women have played a very important part in western culture—both religious and secular—and continue to do so.

A similar assumption has often been made by many historians about the contributions of African-Americans to the history of the United States. Because they were slaves and therefore culturally deprived, it was assumed that black persons had no contribution to make. Until recently, the achievements of African-Americans were rarely recognized in history books about the United States. Gay men and women are also regaining their history after many centuries of silence. Formerly it was assumed by many historians, theologians, and psychologists that they had not made any significant contribution to society and could be ignored, unless of course they gained notoriety as did Oscar Wilde. But historical studies have shown that homosexual persons have made important contributions to human history and culture, contributions that have been ignored by historians because they did not fit into their unexamined set of presuppositions.[7]

"Facts" can be ignored when they do not fit into our way of experiencing the world. In other words, "facts" are dependent upon our personal judgments, our personal subjectivity, and our understanding of ourselves in relationship to our world. They are not as objective as we might like to think. Similarly the "facts of revelation" are also not as objective as we might like to think, for they too are filtered through the experience of God of particular people in their own time and according to their own view of the world in which they lived.

Nowadays, we are much more explicitly conscious of how human beings interact with one another and how our self-understanding is affected by how other people react to us. We live in a post-Freudian age, so that it is much more difficult for us to be unaware of the motivations, desires, and judgments that arise out of the complex human psyche. Several examples come to mind that affect our interpretation of Christian spirituality in the past. Extremes of asceticism, for example, which were once understood as heroic acts of self-denial or martyrdom—and indeed they may well have been—are now interpreted in medical and psychological terms. Heroic acts of fasting might now be seen as symptoms of anorexia, and a willingness to sacrifice one's life for Christ as a martyr can also be understood as a form of suicide.

People, of course, have generally felt the same way in human history, as one can see in any classical literature—they suffered, loved, rejoiced, feared death, and all the other conditions common to human life. Some of the great writers on the spiritual life, such as John of the Cross and Teresa of Avila, have explored the psychological dimensions of their spirituality. Both dealt with their sexuality in very explicit terms, as did Bernard of Clairvaux in his meditations on the Song of Songs, delivered to a community of celibate monks.[8] All of them recognized that their experience as human beings affected the way in which they understood their relationship to God. John of the Cross could speak of God as a Lover who ravished him and entered the secret recesses of his heart:

> O guiding night
> O night more lovely than the dawn!
> O night that has united
> The Lover with His beloved,
> Transforming the beloved in her Lover.
>
> Upon my flowering breast
> Which I kept wholly for Him alone
> There He lay sleeping,
> And I caressing Him
> There in a breeze from the fanning cedars.

When the breeze blew from the turret
Parting His hair,
He wounded my neck
With His gentle hand
Suspending all my senses.

I abandoned and forgot myself,
Laying my face on my Beloved;
All things ceased; I went out from myself;
Leaving my cares
Forgotten among the lilies.[9]

The eroticism of the poem speaks profoundly of John's experience of God in very personal terms.

But generally speaking this sense of individual experience did not dominate classical theology, and more often than not it was not articulated as clearly as we might articulate it today. It was not until the development of a sense of individuality in western culture that the idea of one's own personal experience and way of looking at the world began to be of importance in the understanding of God. The historian Jacob Burckhardt has shown, for example, how a sense of individual identity began to develop during the Renaissance. At that time many people, at least among the leisured and intellectual classes, began to think of the individual in a new way—as "a work of art."[10] The rediscovery of classical literature, a greater sense of personal freedom and equality in society, and a questioning of ecclesiastical authority all contributed to the awareness of one's self as an identity to be cultivated and groomed, rather than as imposed from without, by society or the church.

Another fascinating study has shown how the developing sense of individuality led to changes in the structure of domestic dwellings. As people came to understand themselves as individuals, a greater demand for personal privacy also became important. Unlike the more communal dwellings of earlier centuries, when entire families and even the servants and domestic animals occupied a single room, the more prosperous seventeenth-century families had their own quarters for sleeping or dining.[11] A new question began to dominate western society: who am I as an individual? I know what society thinks of me, but how do I think of myself? What role does my experience of myself play in how I understand my world?

Similar questions are being asked today by women, African-Americans, gay men, and lesbians. Their questions are not simply part of the "decline of western civilization," as some critics of contemporary society might like to think, but rooted in the past several centuries of western culture, and beyond that in the foundations of western society. I once had a conversation with a person who was complaining about the decline of western civilization and culture. The man said, "The Huns are at our gates and we must fight them off." I replied by saying, "We are the children of the Huns; they were our ancestors, and we are the product of their transformation of classical civilization. Perhaps the new 'Huns' will transform our culture just as radically to produce a new and even richer culture."

Such a way of thinking can be very disturbing to many people, and for that reason I think it is necessary to look, however briefly, at the philosophical and theological origins of this shift in western thinking. Philosophers and theologians do not work and think in a vacuum. Rather, they make articulate what other

people in their culture are thinking and feeling—
painters, poets, and musicians, as well as politicians,
and just ordinary people like most of us. They attempt
to analyze critically what is going on in the human
condition and in human belief about God and the
world.[12]

■ **2** ■

Two philosophers in the eighteenth and nineteenth
centuries had an especially significant impact upon
the way in which contemporary theology and human
self-understanding have developed. They were especially important in the analysis of personal experience,
the area concerning us here: Immanuel Kant at the
end of the eighteenth century, and G.W.F. Hegel at the
beginning of the nineteenth. Both philosophers are
complex and difficult to understand; it has been said
that one can only begin to make sense of their writings
on the third reading. But they are crucial to the
development of our concept of experience and of the
human person in modern theology.

Of course, not all contemporary theologians and
philosophers would agree about their importance.
There are theologians, for example, who place a great
emphasis upon the radical distance between God and
humanity. Karl Barth and those who stand in his
tradition are contemporary examples. Barth came out
of a Calvinistic theological position that emphasized
human creatureliness and sin, so that any attempt to
move from an analysis of the human condition to an
understanding of God could only be accounted as hu-

bris or pride. For Barth, God is utterly transcendent and can only be approached through God's revelation in Jesus Christ. Consequently Barth's major emphasis is upon the radical breaking in of God as the word of judgment upon human sin and arrogance. Only the Word revealed to us in Scripture can tell us about God, and only those names for God given to us in Scripture, such as Father and Lord, can be authoritative. But for those of us who believe that the analysis of the human condition—how human beings think of themselves—has importance for our understanding of God, Kant and Hegel can help us articulate more clearly the shift in modern consciousness away from a hierarchically structured view of God and the world to one more concerned with the human person in relationship to God.[13]

Two questions dominated a great deal of philosophical and, to a somewhat lesser degree, theological thinking (theologians always tend to be a bit behind the times) in these two centuries. The first question concerned our knowledge of the empirical world: how could we have certain knowledge about the world that the empirical sciences were so rapidly discovering? The second question asked, how could we understand ourselves and others in a world that was increasingly viewed in empirical and materialistic terms? Many people today ask similar questions about their existence in a world dominated by technology: how do I fit into a world dominated by machines and computers? Formerly, the presupposition of much classical Christian theology was that the world is created and governed by a personal God. God can be approached in prayer and worship; our prayers, together with the intercessions of the saints, have a real effect upon the course of human events. God can at one time be stern and forbidding, compassionate and loving, ready to intervene on our behalf. Most important of all, classical Christian theology and piety assumed that God intervened personally in Jesus Christ in order to redeem human beings from their sin. The church existed as the place where God's personal presence and care could be known and called upon.

Yet the rapid development of science led to another view of the world, one that saw it as an efficient machine, governed by laws, and one allowing little room for a personal—or even, one might say—friendly God. Although Isaac Newton considered himself a Christian, his mechanical model of the workings of the natural order ruled out any necessity for God, except as the one who established the laws of nature in the beginning and "got things moving."

In reaction to such a mechanistic view, Kant and Hegel began to explore the place of the human person in the world. They asked: what is a human being, and how does this being relate to the universe and to God? Hegel even began to explore the notion of the importance of the human community in relation to God, instead of the emphasis upon individualism in the nineteenth century—a concept later developed by Karl Marx. I shall return to that important point in a moment.

The scientific methodology that began to emerge in the eighteenth century tended to limit genuine human knowledge to the empirical: to what could be known through the senses, or empirical knowledge. Here again one of the major presuppositions of classical

Christian piety and theology was being called into question. For earlier Christians it would almost be true to say that what could *not* be known empirically was more important, indeed more real, than what could be known through the senses. Were not the bread and wine of the sacrament of the eucharist, after all, simply signs of a greater reality—the Body and Blood of Christ? And were not the things of this world only signs directing us to the unseen God? Kant was far from returning to such a piety and theology, but he seriously questioned the limitation of our human knowledge only to what could be observed, measured, and quantified. He sought to expand and broaden the scope of human knowledge so that understanding, reason, and what he called "practical reason," or moral judgments, could be seen to have a greater role in our knowledge of the world, ourselves, and God than the empirical sciences would allow.

Kant achieved this not by abandoning the empirical method of science, but by showing that empirical knowledge can only be true knowledge when it is understood by the act of judgment the mind makes through concepts and categories. What was especially important about Kant's philosophical explorations was his analysis of what he called the "transcendental ego," that sense of personal identity through which the varied world of our experience is held together by an "I" that allows me to say "I know" or, in the case of moral judgments, "I will act in this way rather than another." Many things happen to us from the earliest moments of self-consciousness in childhood until our death, and we change in many ways, but we are still conscious of a personal identity through it all. At the age of ten and again at eighty I can still say "I" and maintain some sense of the personal identity out of which I speak, an identity transcending all that has happened to me, even while it is shaped by what has happened to me. This is what Kant meant by the transcendental ego.

Kant's philosophical analysis of the importance of the "I," or transcendental ego, meant that the human person could be thought of not just as a bundle of impressions, but as the personal center through which all our impressions of a world outside ourselves are integrated. To be an "I," to be able to say "I know" or "I will" is to be a person, a center of consciousness with a personal identity. The importance of Kant's analysis of the transcendental ego is most obvious to those who, while they may not be interested in philosophical questions, have to make moral choices. Making a serious moral choice means to be able to say "*I*" take responsibility for what I am doing. Those who for some reason cannot take responsibility for what they do are not considered to be moral agents by most moral and legal codes. It is with this sense of the person that Kant is concerned: the personal center out of which I am able to say "I will" or "I will not" act in a.certain way.

But his analysis of the transcendental ego has implications also for what we know and believe about the world in which we live. One of the pervading questions asked by philosophers—who tend to ask strange questions—is: what do I know when I know anything? The question is strange because most of us, most of the time, do not reflect upon what it means to *know* something; we simply do it. But at times the question can become vitally important—when, for example, we have to distinguish between what we are simply aware of and what those impressions *mean*. In other words, when we have to distinguish between what we see or hear, and what those impressions tell us about the world.

Some of the impressions we receive from our sense experience are important and some are not. What makes the difference? I may hear a piece of music simply as a collection of noises, but if I am a musician I can hear in these noises themes, variations, and harmonies that are the structure, or meaning, of the music. In other words, the sounds have a pattern; they are not merely random noises. In a similar way, all good preachers or teachers know that they have to make sense out of a great deal of raw data if they are to communicate. What were the important, crucial events which led up to a war or a revolution? The historian is able to say, "These are the important facts; the others are unimportant." Whether or not the historian is correct in his or her judgment will reflect the depth of learning that lies behind the judgment itself. A good preacher can read the morning paper and be able to see how certain events relate to the Gospel, while others do not.

So to say "I know something" is to say that by an act of my mind I can understand what is happening and arrange my impressions so that they make some sense. This is something we do all the time, even though we may not consciously be aware of what we are doing. I may have many feelings and bits of information about God or the world, but in order to communicate them to others I must order them in a conceptual way. I must be able to say that *I know* this to be the case. The "I" is the unity of all the impressions given to me through the senses and my conceptual ordering of those impressions. This is what Kant means by experience; that unity of understanding and sense impressions that makes knowledge possible. The "I" that knows is the personal subject, the center of my existence as a person. But as I said earlier, Kant's analysis of the act of the personal subject in knowing and acting did not emerge out of his idle speculation. It reflected the shift in self-consciousness from the corporate to the individual that was taking place in human awareness of the self.

In the next century Hegel built upon the foundation that Kant had laid. He greatly expanded our understanding of what it is to be a person through his analysis of our experience—not only of sense objects in general, but also of other persons in particular. For as intelligent, conscious beings, we know and come into relationship with other persons, other conscious beings. In his *Phenomenology of Mind*,[14] which many think to be his most obscure and (perhaps for that reason) greatest book, Hegel sought to show how our relationship with other persons is actually the process through which we become conscious of ourselves. Through such relationships we can move beyond the isolation of our own individuality in which the individual *self* is the only thing that really matters. As I experience someone else—whether that "other" be another person or ultimately God—I come to a sense of myself (Hegel calls it self-consciousness) that allows me to experience another person (or God) not as an object "out there some place," but in the depth of myself in and through my communion with others. The term Hegel uses to describe this process of experience is transcendence—my transcendence of myself (as one who is isolated from others in my individuality) into communion with others.

Transcendence does not mean loss of self or a corporate merger with a higher reality in which I lose my identity—as so often happens with corporate mergers in the business world. It is rather a process through which I come to a deeper understanding of who I truly am, a deeper sense of my own identity. For Hegel and for much modern theology, this process is called dialectic. Dialectic is a process of thinking and acting through which we come to understand how the truth of anything whatsoever—its reality—is not just its *self-identity*, but its identity in relationship. The truth is not simply expressed in a single proposition nor in one proposition in isolation from others. To say, "This is another human being" is only to express one small aspect of who and what this person is. To know the truth about another person is to engage in a dialectical process that is really a journey of discovery, in which one aspect of the truth is known through its relation to other truths about the person.

This notion of dialectic that Hegel developed is really quite simple, but, as with so many simple notions, difficult to express. I shall try to illustrate what he means. If I want to describe a good friend to someone else, I can say many things about him: what he looks like, what things he enjoys, how he feels about issues. While each statement may be true, no one of them can fully describe the whole reality of my friend. Additionally, some of the statements may seem to be both positive and negative. My friend may be very stubborn and unwilling to see other points of view; he may also be a person of very strong convictions, one who will fight for what he believes is right. In other words, no one statement can fully and truthfully describe him; the *truth* about my friend will call for many different statements. And no matter how much I may say about my friend, there will always be a mystery about him, something that cannot be fully articulated. My knowledge of the "truth" about him, his reality, will always be for me and for him a "journey of discovery." In a homey way—Hegel is much more complicated—this is what the dialectical process involves. To see the truth about anything whatsoever is also to see that the truth is multifaceted.

Such dialectical knowing is also, of course, true about our relationship with God. No one set of statements, or even many sets of statements, can ever fully express the reality we believe God to be; God is always beyond any proposition we might make about the divine nature. For that reason we must always talk about God dialectically, that is, we must attempt to understand how one name or way of talking about God calls forth another name or way of talking.

Such a dialectic is common in the Old Testament. God's wrath towards the people of Israel, for example, is always balanced by talk of God's mercy and forgiveness—that God has "repented" of the divine wrath. In most cases this contrast represents the work of different editors of the original material, because a later editor of the earlier narrative found it inappropriate to think of God as wrathful. And sometimes it represented a new insight into the course of events: God

might threaten Israel with destruction for its trans-
gression, but that prediction about God's purpose did
not come to pass. Consequently, a subsequent editor
had to correct the original judgment. However, such
passages became in due course a received part of the
scriptural tradition.

In much the same way, I may at one time in my life
feel God's wrath, but at a later time I may be able to
see that wrath is also mercy and forgiveness. Such a
journey of discovery into God is dialectical. It recognizes that how I understand God at a particular point
in my own life does not fully express the being of God.
Oftentimes, then, one way of naming God can call
forth another name as we continue on our journey into
God. To call God our father can also call forth the
image of God as our mother, the one who nurtures and
cares for us. The two names do not exclude one
another. Rather, they express the dialectical nature of
all of our language about God.

Indeed, our names and concepts express the dialectical nature of our relationship with God, just as they do
about our relationships with other people. In my communion with other people and with God, I come to
know at the deepest level of my existence that I am a
limited, fragile, and mortal person, one who is dependent upon others and cannot really control the world
around me. But it is also to know myself as one who is
able to experience love and freedom in myself and
others. I can enter into the mystery of myself and
others, not in order to control or limit them, but to participate in them and to love them in their freedom.
God is what calls us to transcend ourselves in others,
in order that we may ultimately be found in God. To

experience God, then, is to come to know myself in others. That, I believe, is to express in religious terms what Hegel was seeking to express conceptually and abstractly when he spoke of the dialectic of transcendence.

■ 3 ■

As I have already suggested, the word "experience" is tricky. It can be used in a variety of ways. Some of those ways will be emotional or sentimental, some will attempt to articulate a feeling about someone or something that is difficult to express in precise terms. I have known people to say, for example, that they were able to accept the ordained ministry of women because of the "good experience" they have had of women in the priesthood. In other words, women have been able to minister to them as effectively, if not more so, than many men, and therefore the arguments they had heard against the ordination of women were no longer important; these theological arguments went against their "experience." Some people might want to dismiss such remarks, but really we cannot do so. In the final analysis, no matter how nebulous it may be, the appeal to experience carries great weight. It has been used throughout Christian history as the foundation for doctrinal formulations.

There are many examples of the complex dialectic between experience and doctrinal formulations in Christian history. The most obvious, of course, is to be found in the letters of Paul. There we can see Paul struggling with the relationship of Jesus to the God of

Israel. Paul was a good Jew, as he makes abundantly clear in his letter to the Galatians and the sermons reported in the Acts of the Apostles. But, as he also makes clear in many of his letters, in Jesus Christ Paul *experienced* salvation. In Jesus Christ he came to know that he was justified before God and that he was freed from the Law. His experience of Christ on the road to Damascus was only the beginning of his deepening awareness that in Jesus Christ he was justified by faith: "for in Christ Jesus you are all sons of God, through faith" (Gal. 3:26)—all of us can call God Abba because now we know God through Jesus Christ.

To experience salvation in Christ meant, of course, that Jesus was somehow related to God and, therefore, not just another prophet. The theological question for Paul was: how can we reconcile Jesus, the man who saves, with the God of Israel? But Paul appears to have been reluctant simply to identify Jesus with God, and therefore his way of talking about the relationship is always somewhat ambiguous. In the opening salutation of his letter to the Romans, for example, Paul refers to Jesus as the Son of God, "who was descended from David according to the flesh and designated Son of God in power according to the Spirit of holiness by his resurrection from the dead" (Rom. 1:3-4). In other words, Paul experienced God in Jesus Christ, but he also began the church's struggle to understand how the experience of salvation in Jesus could be an experience of God. In the continuing experience of the church, the relationship of Christ and the Spirit to God did become more fully articulated in doctrinal and liturgical terms, yet the need for greater articulation arose always out of the experience of salvation in Christ and the Spirit.

So then, because the relationship is so complex, we must attempt to define the word "experience" more precisely if we are to speak of it as the source of our naming of God. Our words for God, whether they be metaphors or concepts, derive from our experience. What then does this central and important term mean?

Experience, as I understand it, is a process in which all of us engage all the time. It is a process by which we create and discover a world of meaning for ourselves. To be a human being, someone who thinks about and reflects upon what happens, requires that we understand the significance, the meaning, of what is happening. A dog or a cat, no matter how "intelligent" it may be, reacts to situations on the basis of instinctive or learned behavior. A human being tries, in most cases, to understand what a situation means in order to react appropriately, even though many of our reactions appear to be instinctive or simply habitual. When I open my eyes to the world around me, when I see, touch, taste, and hear, I attempt to categorize, to name, and to define it. I know that a chair is something I can sit on, but that a fragile antique table is something I shouldn't sit on, lest there be unfortunate consequences. What is even more important, I can learn the difference between the two. All of those judgments are perfectly ordinary in everyday life, but they are also of great significance, for they enable us to define and name our world, to know what we can do and what we cannot do, to discover and also to create its meaning for us.

Involved in this process are two factors: the knowledge given us through our senses and the ideas we form about this information. Both are necessary if we are to talk about experience as something other than our instinctive reactions—if we are to talk about it and name it in relationship to a world with content and meaning.

There are, however, two other dimensions of experience that are equally important. Not only do I understand and name the objects and situations that enter my consciousness from the world around me— my individual experience, in other words—but I also share in the history of the experiences of other human beings through language, stories, music, and painting. One of the reasons why it is so difficult to learn another language, for example, is that it is hard for us to understand the verbal associations and the history of certain forms of speech, even though we may know what a word means. Words carry with them a history of the experience of many generations of people. At one point in my life when I was struggling to learn Spanish, I would frequently discover that a perfectly ordinary dictionary translation was totally inadequate to express my meaning, because the associations were different.

The most obvious example of the problem is in our naming of God. While it is true that I name God to a considerable degree out of my personal encounter with God in prayer, I also share in the history of other people's encounter with God. For the Christian, of course, that history begins with the Old and New Testaments and continues in the theological and worshiping tradition of the church. My experience is a shared experience in the community of those who have believed, and who will continue to believe long after I am dead. I can name God, and I can name my world, only as I have received from others the language, images, stories, and poetry of the past. In turn, I share in the creation of experience for others in the future as a teacher, preacher, and story-teller. I must locate my individual experience within the larger context of the history of Christian experience as it has been expressed doctrinally and liturgically.

In ecumenical conversations among the various Christian churches, we are slowly (and sometimes painfully) beginning to learn that Christians from different traditions have their own experience of what it means to be a Christian. I have been a participant in many ecumenical conversations, and one of the most important things I have learned is that my way of talking about the "experience" of God's saving work in Christ is not definitive. The salvation I know may be the same, but my experience of it as an Anglican can be quite different from that of, say, a Lutheran. I express my experience of salvation in sacramental and liturgical forms, whereas a Lutheran will express it in doctrinal forms. As contact increases with other, non-Christian traditions, with their own history and language, we Christians will have to ask ourselves how our language, which describes our history with God, is related to the history of other peoples. Is the name "God" one that can be understood in the same way by the Christian and non-Christian peoples of Africa and Asia, who have had a different history of the experience of God?

Another dimension we must also keep in mind is that experience is more than our reaction to the world in which we live. It also involves the world we are creating for ourselves as we interpret and understand it. Experience involves experimentation. When I enter into a serious relationship, such as friendship or marriage, a relationship involving much more than just the physical presence of another person, I reach out to discover who that person is, what she feels and believes in. When I casually encounter another person in a crowded train or airplane, I may very well ignore him, but when that person begins to mean something to me, then I want to know whether this is someone who can have significance in my life. The beginning of any valuable human relationship is a form of experimentation, a process of discovery through which I can come to experience some dimensions of the reality of another person, and learn what he or she is like. Experience in ordinary life is experimental; it is a form of education.

Nowhere, I believe, is this sense of experience as experimentation more obvious than in our relationship with God. The "experience of God" in prayer is always a testing of God. When I was a child, I tested God in my prayers to see whether or not God would give me what I wanted for Christmas. As an adult, I still test God to see whether or not God will live up to my expectations. One of the delights, for example, of reading the Psalms is to realize how the Psalmist is challenging God, calling the divine actions into question, and even bargaining with God. The Psalmist thinks nothing of calling God's actions into question, as in Psalm 80, where he rebukes God for neglecting the people of

Israel, or in Psalm 88, which expresses his anger against God because of God's enmity towards him.

To experience God, as to experience another person, is to enter into a creative relationship rather than a passive one. It is the probing of a mystery. I name God out of my experience of God—the testing, the thanksgiving, the anger I feel when I think God has not given me what I need. I can have all those feelings towards my parents or towards friends. They are an important part of my experience, and they express how I am growing in my experience of others. So too with God. To experience God is to be in a relationship that is always changing and deepening.

Moses and Jesus, we believe, experienced God in the most radical and transforming way, and out of their experience they named God: "I Am" and "Father." The names arising out of their experience have become fundamental to our belief in God and what we believe the divine nature to be. But both Jews and Christians continue to have the experience of God in their lives, and out of that continuing experience we too seek to name God. Indeed, we must continue to do so, because the "experience of God" is not something that happened only in the past. We must give meaning to our present experience, if the name "God" is once again to be a name of holiness and power, a name that calls people to belief, showing them what it means to be truly human, living in relationship with the God who is the meaning of all that is.

CHAPTER V
The Way of Naming

▪ 1 ▪

In previous chapters, we have looked at those areas in our naming of God that are fundamental to Christian people: the biblical tradition and its authority, our prayer and worship, and our personal experience of God as transcendent mystery. In all these areas, the names we use to speak to or about God carry with them images of the God about whom we speak. Language carries with it the history of the images and concepts which human beings have of God.

Now many of the images and concepts which those names convey are being challenged. Many non-western Christians claim that their experience of God in prayer and liturgical worship and their reading of Holy Scripture lead them to call God by other names, names that express their cultural heritage. The Christian who has been raised in an explicitly polytheistic culture will "hear" the credal confession of God as "the one God" differently than will those of us who have only known what it is to believe in one God—the God of the Judaeo-Christian tradition. Such Christians need to name the one God in reference to the gods that still may dominate the lives of their families and friends. I have known this to be true of Christians in Haiti, where the gods of the Haitian-African heritage must still be acknowledged, and sometimes even feared and placated, in religious ceremonies. To do this is not to deny the one God, but to recognize a cultural heritage that cannot simply be cast to one side. The Christian God must, therefore, be named as the God who has ultimate power over the gods who still figure in the lives of others, and who may still linger in one's own religious consciousness.

In order to explore the issues that are being raised for us, we must look more carefully at the way in which we go about naming God, that is to say, how our names of God stand in relation to the other names we use in our ordinary experience of the world. Certainly we cannot abandon the names for God that have come to us in the biblical, liturgical, and theological tradition, but it may be possible for us to understand how our way, as western Christians, both male and female, should be more open to other possibilities from other cultures, as well as other possibilities from our own. What I want to explore, then, is how our names for God, whether they be images or concepts, arise from experiences of God that are not limited to, or defined by, a perspective that is chiefly western, white, and male. The time has come to explore other kinds of experience.

We use proper names or nouns to name objects that are common in our experience. We refer to David or Sarah when we are talking about another human being; we have names for our dogs and cats. But naming God is somewhat different. David and Sarah, dogs and cats, we can see, touch, and experience in a way we cannot experience God. No one has seen or touched God. Our naming of God is different from our naming of people or animals. We must, therefore, name God differently—it must be a way of naming based on our experience of God, yet not dependent upon our seeing or touching or hearing. While many people have claimed to have had visions of God or to have heard God, we recognize that those experiences have a character different from our ordinary vision or hearing. They require a different kind of language in order to describe them: the language of poetry or saga, for example, such as we find in so much of the Old Testament. There the experience of God is described as a still small voice or a mighty wind—images that we would not ordinarily use of our experience of other human beings, dogs and cats, or objects such as trees. Naming God out of our experience is, in other words, different from naming a child or a pet or a live oak.

There are two ways of naming God I want to look at. Both arise out of our experience, and both are essential to how we understand the world in which we live and the God whom we encounter in personal prayer and liturgical worship. Both are to be found in Scripture and in the theological tradition of the church. Both forms of language are necessary in our ordinary dealing with our experience, and both are necessary in our naming of God.

The first, metaphorical language, primarily uses images. It describes the things we experience in images that have great power to move us and enable us to appreciate more fully what we are experiencing. In the Bible, God is described or named in many images: a Rock, a Shepherd, or a King. All of those metaphors are familiar to us from our everyday speech.

The second way, because it is conceptual and abstract, is more difficult to describe. It is known as analogical language, and it expresses our experience of the world and God in terms of ideas and concepts, as when we say that God is good or just or merciful. We also use such language in ordinary conversation, saying, for example, that a political cause is good because we believe it will lead to greater justice for the oppressed.

Imagistic language about God frequently takes the form of metaphor. It brings together different images that we normally might not associate with one another, but that in their juxtaposition can give us a new insight into both. For example, to say that God is a judge is to relate our ordinary experience of judges as those who dispense justice to the idea of God as the dispenser of justice. Not all human judges, alas, hand out justice with complete fairness; they can be influenced by ordinary human passion. Yet we believe God's justice to be both merciful and fair. Thus, metaphorical language can lead to a more comprehensive understanding of God as one who can be talked about in human terms.

The philosopher Aristotle long ago made the fundamental definition of metaphorical language, when he described metaphor as the transferred use of a term that properly belongs to something else, as when we say that a ship *stands* in the harbor.[1] Ships do not "stand" in the same way that human beings or animals do, but the juxtaposition of the images can help us to see what a ship in the harbor is doing. Aristotle's seemingly simple definition has given rise to many complex discussions by rhetoricians, philosophers, and theologians. In her important and creative book *Models of God*, theologian Sallie McFague expands the notion of metaphor as a primary way of talking about God when she uses the image of God as Friend. To think of God as a friend rather than as a parent can have great power, as I suggested in an earlier chapter. It can convey to us a totally different image of God. All the various theories about metaphor point to the fact that we can explain one thing by referring to something else. We are able to see through the metaphor something we might otherwise have missed, or only perceived with a great deal of explanation.[2]

In Scripture, especially in the Psalms, there are many vivid images for God. Some are similes describing God as a stronghold, a crag, or a haven, or the savior of the poor, or the one who makes the earth tremble or whose voice strips the forest bare. Others are metaphors in the proper sense, such as Father, Shepherd, and King. They are metaphors drawn from different situations and conditions in Jewish and early Christian experience. The Jews, for example, were originally a nomadic people, moving about with their flocks, so that it was easy for them to think of God as a shepherd, one who cares for the people of Israel as a shepherd cares for his sheep. This metaphor appears often not only in the Psalms, but also in Ezekiel, where God is described as the shepherd of Israel (see especially 14:7-8, 10b-11). Later, in Hebrews, Jesus is described as the great shepherd of the sheep (13:20). The image of God or Jesus as a shepherd expresses the particular care God has for the people of the Old Covenant and the New.[3]

Jews were also a people who depended, as most ancient peoples did, upon a family structure as the basis of society. Consequently, to speak of God in parental terms came quite naturally. God could care for the people as a father and mother care for their children. The prophet Amos also speaks of Israel as God's family, and Hosea speaks of Israel as a woman who has betrayed her husband. At a later time in their history the people of Israel, when they began living in towns and cities, began to think of God as a king or ruler. 1 Samuel tells the story of God's anger when Israel demanded a king, rather than a judge to rule over them. Yahweh says to Samuel: "They have not rejected you, but they have rejected me from being king over them....You shall solemnly warn them, and show them the ways of the king who shall reign over them" (1 Sam. 8:7-9). Even though the image of king would predominate in later writings of the Old Testament and continue into the New, Yahweh's anger suggests that even though God acquiesced to this demand, the name King was not initially pleasing. The names Israel used, in other words, reflected a history and imaged the way they understood their relationship with God. The names could change as their experience of themselves and of God changed.

Some of the metaphors the Israelites used to describe their experience of God can be problematic for us many centuries later. For example, it is difficult for those who have never known sheep, or have never seen a shepherd, to realize that shepherding the sheep of Israel was not an easy job. Sheep are not affectionate, woolly lambs, as we might like to think them to be, and as we might even like to think of ourselves; they can be stubborn, raunchy, and belligerent. A shepherd's job is not an easy one.[4] So for us to think of God or Jesus as a shepherd tending woolly lambs can be a most misleading image of God or of Jesus, causing us to lose sight of the cantankerous nature of human beings and the difficult life of shepherds. I have not had the experience of being a shepherd, but I have seen shepherds in some of the more barren parts of Spain, suffering from heat and isolation while guarding their flocks. The metaphor of God as shepherd spoke much more strongly to me after I had seen a real one.

There are many other metaphors and images in Scripture. To say that God is our rock is to express in a meaningful image that God is steadfast, there from the beginning, firm, a place of refuge from the storm, something onto which we can climb and hold fast. All those meanings are conveyed to us and evoke a reaction in us when we refer to God as the "Rock of Ages." Similarly, to speak of God as father or mother conveys and evokes a relationship that otherwise would take many words to describe. As I have discussed earlier, some of the feelings those parental names call up may not always be appropriate to the relationship we have with God at a particular time. At other times, however, they may speak to us strongly of God as one who nurtures and cares for us.

Metaphors are fundamental to our experience of the world, of other people, of ourselves, and of God. Metaphors do not give us hard bits of data; they are not mere facts, in other words. Of course, all facts need to be interpreted and understood. They are not isolated from the rest of our experience, but always possess a

context in which they must be understood. But metaphors enable us to take the hard bits of data—what is
given to us in our sense experience and what we like to
think of as factual knowledge—and see the relationships that things have with one another.

Our metaphors *for* God are fundamental to our experience *of* God. They help us relate what we know
about our world—whether rocks or shepherds or
mothers—to the God who transcends us and is hidden
from our sight. God is not a "fact." We cannot deal with
God as we deal with the things of our ordinary experience. But metaphors express the history out of
which we have come in our experience of God, a history expressed in stories, songs, poetry, and myths.
They express our movement towards God, our probing
of the mystery. Just as a metaphor enables us to "see"
the relationship of finite temporal things to one
another, so it enables us to "see" the relationship of
finite and temporal things to those that are not.

One of the richest metaphors in the New Testament,
for instance, is Jesus' comparison of himself to the
Temple in Jerusalem (John 2:19). In the religious life
of the Jews the Temple had a deep significance. It was
the place where God dwelt, and the rebuilding of the
Temple after its destruction was of great importance—
it signified God's presence. When the gospel writers
refer to Jesus as the Temple ("Destroy this temple, and
in three days I will raise it up"), they are in effect
identifying him with the presence of God, the place
where the Torah, the Law, is to be found. A metaphor
like that could be said to be irreducible, because it
says something that could not be said in any other
way. We who do not know our Bible very well will not

hear all of the allusions, but even for us the metaphor calls up the history of the Jewish people and the importance of the Temple in their tradition.

There are similar irreducible metaphors in all religious language, but the most important and most obvious for us are those associated with the Christian sacraments of baptism and eucharist. To speak of the water of baptism, for example, calls forth the whole history of our relationship to God as we know it in Jesus Christ. Perhaps because the Jewish people and the early Christians lived in a sparse and arid land, the image of water figures largely in Scripture. But water is also fundamental to human life. We all need water in order to survive. As most scientists would now say, we human beings, and all other animals, came from the water. And indeed most people seek out the oceans or lakes for their annual holidays. There is something about water which both strengthens and comforts us.

But there is more to the water of baptism than merely a return to the primal elements. In the Old Testament there is the story of the flood with which God cleansed the earth. Early Christians, such as the writer of 1 and 2 Peter, used the image of the flood and the ark in order to signify the church as the ark of salvation. When the people of Israel were wandering in the desert, Moses struck a rock and water gushed forth. Jesus himself calmed a storm at sea and even, we are told, walked on the water to demonstrate his power over it. All of those images, and there are many more, come together when we speak of the water of baptism. In baptism, we are not only washed of our sins but made new, brought into a new relationship

with God, and incorporated into the church. As the
Book of Common Prayer says: "We thank you,
Almighty God, for the gift of water. Over it the Holy
Spirit moved in the beginning of creation....We thank
you for the water of baptism. In it we are buried with
Christ in his death. By it we share in his resurrection.
Through it we are reborn by the Holy Spirit."[5]

Similarly, the metaphor of the body of Christ that is
so central to the eucharist calls forth many allusions:
the body of Jesus born to Mary, the body which was
offered on the cross, the body of the risen Lord, the
body which was exalted to the "right hand of the
Father." All of those images are called forth when we
speak of the church as "the Body of Christ," or when in
the eucharist the celebrant speaks of "the Body of
Christ, the Bread of heaven." To understand the metaphor of the church as the body of Christ is to see the
link between our communion within the body of the incarnate Christ, our personal status as temples of God,
in whom the Spirit dwells, and our communion with
the body that is the church—that is, our dying and rising again, our adoption as sons and daughters of God.
The body born of Mary takes the form of the eucharistic body in order that it may exist in the body of
Christ, the church.

The history of God with all of God's people is expressed in such metaphors and could not be expressed
in any other way. These metaphors draw upon our history, and they express our relationship to mystery;
they express our life with God, our experience of God.
Some of the metaphors and names we derive from that
history are irreducible and more powerful than others,
and so they always need to be reexamined in every

generation of the church's life, in order to see if they are still capable of holding significant meaning for us. But certainly any language we use about God will always involve the figurative, and it will always use metaphors and images drawn from human experience.

▪ 2 ▪

As important as such language may be, however, there are certain problems with it that we do not always recognize. The human tendency is often to lose a sense of the mystery of God by our domestication of the divine. The most extreme form of this tendency is idolatry, when we attempt to use God through magic or manipulation. The story is told—I do not know its source—that a priest was once known to say that he was more powerful than God, because when he said the words of consecration in the eucharist, God had to come down from heaven! In a more subtle way, we can also lose sight of the mystery when we idolize one set of images or metaphors, and forget that they are conditioned and modified by the total experience of people with God; consequently they may not be as absolute as we think. They may, in fact, be influenced by context, by time and place, as well as by the personal experience of the peoples from which they derive. As I said in an earlier chapter, revelation in Scripture depended upon a human being responding to God and hearing the divine word. It did not take place in a vacuum, or arbitrarily.

A woman living in the third century BCE, in a society where her role was limited to caring for a family and household, would understand herself and her relationship to God quite differently than a professional woman of the twentieth century. Even though they might share many things in common, some of the metaphors and images of Scripture would speak to them quite differently. A woman who for professional reasons has decided not to marry and bear children might find it difficult to identify with this experience, yet this is the dominant picture of women in Scripture. When the men are out fighting, the women stay at home tending the hearth. Not all men or women would be able to identify themselves as warriors or homemakers. Many years ago, I moved into an apartment in which there was no kitchen because, as the architect said, "Men don't cook." I quickly corrected that stereotype by having a kitchen installed and inviting his wife and him to dinner. I do not see myself as a warrior, just as many women do not see themselves as cooks. But such images are dominant in Scripture.

In *Models of God*, Sallie McFague has argued for metaphor as the primary way for us to speak of God and to understand our relationship with God and with the world. She believes that the male-dominated language of Scripture and theology has resulted in our insensitivity to the environment in which we live—one of domination. Instead she proposes the metaphors of Mother, Lover, and Friend for the trinity of God.

While similar images and metaphors abound in Holy Scripture and in liturgical language, the problem is that they, too, are grounded in the materiality of time and space. They fall short of a complete conceptual understanding of God. Yet we sometimes need a conceptual language about God if we are to name God in a way that can enable us to communicate what we believe to those who may not understand or respond to personal or time-bound images and metaphors.

Because a metaphor is the carrying over or transfer of the meaning of one term to another, figurative language can strike the imagination and intelligence. It can stretch our use of words and images when used of God, but it can also limit what we have to say about God to the physicality or materiality of the metaphor and its particular history. Thus to say that "God is my king" may either be a meaningless metaphor—as it certainly is for most people today, who do not know what kingship means—or one that evokes images of oppression, as it certainly did to the leaders of the American Revolution. Metaphor, while certainly a necessary way of talking about God, shares much in the imperfections of created things, and does not allow us to talk about the perfections in God, such as Justice, Truth, Goodness. These are matters we need to talk about if we are to speak of God to a culture that thinks of God, or even feels about God, in a sentimental and anthropomorphic way—God is my "co-pilot," to recall a popular song during World War II. As one theologian asked in response to Professor McFague's book,

> Is the image of mother or lover, then—any more than the images father and lord—of a sort that can provide an adequate basis for a contemporary understanding of God? Is any *image* sufficiently complex to perform this function? Or is it only when we move to the order of *concepts* that we are able to hold before the mind the sort of complexity with which we are here concerned?[6]

A related problem with metaphor is that it can be limited to a particular culture. If you believe (as I certainly do) that some knowledge of the transcendent mystery that we name "God" is possible to those outside the tradition of biblical revelation, then we must have a language that allows them to understand what we mean when we Christians use the word "God." At the present time, because of increasing dialogue between Christianity and other religious traditions, the particular metaphors and metaphorical names for God that are a part of our history may well need to be expanded and opened up, so that they can accommodate and be illuminated by the names and metaphors found in other traditions. The metaphor of God as the husband of Israel, a husband who expects Israel to be faithful to him, might not speak very clearly to a culture in which polygamy is common, or in which spouses are not expected to be faithful.

An interesting illustration from classical theology shows the same heightened awareness of and appreciation for non-Christian religions we have now. In the thirteenth century, Thomas Aquinas argued that the name or word "God" can have a diversity of meanings and can legitimately be used by both "pagans" and Christians. Some people would argue, he says, that the name "God" can only have one true meaning, claiming there is no relation between the true use of the word by the Christian and the false use of it by the pagans. Aquinas says, however, that the name "God" can have different meanings, deriving from different understandings of the concept of "God," but that they are all related to one another. What this concept means to one group of people has to be understood in relation to what it might mean to another.

Of course, Aquinas believed the Christian use of the word "God" was the most authentic, but his way of analyzing the concept "God" illustrates how the meaning we assign to it may not be confined to a particular context. The metaphorical names we use for God, because they are derived from a socially conditioned experience of God, are less open to other traditions. Even in the thirteenth century Aquinas could recognize that there are a variety of meanings in the concept of God. Conceptual language is important because it allows us to see the lines of connection between Christian belief and that of other religious traditions.

Finally, metaphorical language, because its images are concrete and historical, does not point to what I would call the "negative moment" in all language about God. No matter what we say about God, we need always to remember that we do not know *how* our words about God are true of God, for they are hidden in the mystery of God. We can, perhaps, know how they are true in our terms, but that is not the same thing as knowing how they are true in God. We must never forget that God is a mystery hidden from our eyes, a mystery that can only be known in oblique ways, not directly and certainly. Our language about God must always reflect the mystery with which we are dealing. It must have a "negative quality" about it, a willingness to accept the fact that we do not know everything there is to know about God.

I remember a story told by a friend of mine who was teaching church school on a Sunday morning. He said to his young children, "This morning as I was coming to church, I looked up into a tree and saw a gray, furry animal. What do you think it was?" A child, because she was in church and knew that being in church required a religious answer, said, "Jesus." The furry animal was, of course, a squirrel, but the child was giving the expected answer in the context of Sunday School. The "negative moment" in speaking of God was not yet a factor for her.

The Christian life is always the participation in a mystery about which we cannot be completely and perfectly certain—as hard as it may be for us in the twentieth century to accept such a reality. We are conditioned to believe that we can know everything if we only work at it hard enough. Some Christians would say that we only have to read the Bible, but most of us know that the Bible does not provide all of the answers to our complex questions about abortion, euthanasia, and genetic manipulation. The will of God, like God, remains a mystery to be approached in the quietness and humility of prayer and worship. Yet we must use language about God, language that involves more than our feelings, more than our images. What kind of language is that?

I know what it means to say about another person, "He is just in all his dealings," or "She is a good physician." I have evidence upon which to base both assertions, and I think I know what it means for a person to be "just" or "good." I can make positive assertions about the meaning of justness and goodness in a particular person because I can see the evidence of it in the way in which he or she treats me and other people. But I cannot make such claims in the same way about God, who always surpasses the kind of knowledge that we have about people or things in our ordinary experience. Our language about God is always limited to our way of understanding the world, whether we speak of God in concepts or in images and metaphors.

We can see something of the importance of this if we think of the problem, or better yet the mystery, of pain and suffering—what we call the evil in our world. We say that God is good and wills the good for us, and yet we know that there is much in this world that is horrible. If we truly believe that God is good, how do we understand the evil in the world? If we believe that God is just, how do we understand social and economic injustice? Yet we also believe that somehow all that is wrong in our world will be made right. As Christians who believe in the God who has been revealed in Jesus Christ, we do believe that God is good and just.

In other words, we do not know ultimately what it means to say that God is "just" or "good," and yet we believe that God is both. We do not know what the concepts mean in God except in terms of how we understand them in our own experience. That is why we have so much difficulty in "justifying the ways of God," even though we continue to believe that the terms good and just are true of God. Conceptual language, in other words, exposes the limitations of our way of talking about God. It shows us how limited our language is when dealing with the mystery of God.

Metaphorical language, on the other hand, seems to make more positive assertions. Because of the concreteness of its imagery, it can tempt us to think that we know more about God than we do. It can allow us to confuse the image with the reality. While we obviously would not confuse God with a rock or an earthly king or queen (although that has sometimes happened in human history!), we can, and many have, easily confuse God the Father with our human fathers. Gregory of Nazianzus, along with Thomas Aquinas, for example, argued that the name "Father" is not a metaphor for God because it refers primarily to the relationships of the Trinity, not to a nature or an essence. But however much theologians might insist, most people who call God "Father" think of human fathers, and thus project onto God both the quality of maleness and their experience with their own fathers. Should the name "Mother" come to be used more frequently in Christian worship, it may well be that many people will begin to confuse God the "Mother" with their own mothers, thereby projecting onto God their feelings, both good and bad, about motherhood. As most people know, especially those who have been involved in any form of counseling, projection can be a serious problem in our relationships. We can project upon our family, friends, and employers our own expectations, anger, frustration, and desires in order to make them into what we think they ought to be. We can do the same thing with God. We can attempt to make God into what we think God ought to be—a father, a mother, or anyone else.

One has to be careful with metaphors when they are used of God; they can often suggest more than we mean them to suggest. As important as they are in liturgical and private prayer, there must always be a sense of the negative. God is not described or defined or categorized by a metaphor or a particular image, but rather we are directed towards the mystery of God by the images we use. We can use different images or metaphors at different times, but they must always be understood for what they are—a way of talking to or about God drawn from our own experience of the world.

What is needed, then, is a corrective to metaphorical language—not an alternative that replaces it, but one that can enrich and clarify it. I have called this corrective conceptual language, which expresses our critical, rational reflection about our experience of God in concepts and ideas. Conceptual language, while it may not be as familiar to those who do not think of themselves as theologians, is necessary if we are to untangle some of the vexed questions involved in naming God. That kind of language is necessary also in our everyday lives. Most people, for example, are familiar with the experience of loving another person and finding that the best way they can describe or talk about their love is through various kinds of metaphors and images. Perhaps the most vivid example of metaphorical and imagistic language can be found in the Song of Songs in the Old Testament—language so erotically intense that Christians have often taken it to describe the relationship between Christ and the church, even though it is a love poem.

But we know also—or at least we ought to know—that the relationship of love must be reflected upon and conceptualized: "Will I be able to live with this person the rest of my life?" "Will this be a person who can help me experience more deeply the grace of God in my life?" Those are questions which, in one form or another, we always need to ask. One way of talking about our experience of another person does not exclude or negate the other. So too in our relationship with God: the experience of God must be expressed in metaphors, but it must also be conceptualized. I must be able to say that God is one to whom I can pray because God reaches out to me in Christ and the Spirit.

▪ 3 ▪

There are several ways in which we can discuss conceptual language about God,[7] but the one I want to put forward here is called analogy or, as it is technically called, analogical predication. Analogy is the attempt to understand the relationship between ourselves and God in conceptual terms through rational analysis. But before we get into that, it might be helpful to see how we use analogy in our ordinary way of talking.

Like metaphorical language, analogical language is something we use quite frequently. We use it whenever we make a comparison between two situations and say that there are certain similarities and certain differences, but the similarities are sufficiently great for us to be able to see the relationship between them. Thus I might say, "There is an analogy between the American Civil War and the English Civil War. In both cases families were divided against themselves, a land-owning class was pitted against a rising mercantile class, and for some time it appeared that the Cavaliers and the Confederacy would be victorious." There are both similarities and differences, but the similarities and the differences can help us to understand both wars somewhat more clearly.

Another example (and one used frequently by Thomas Aquinas, who developed the classic analysis of analogy) would be the use of the word "healthy." When a physician says the medicine she gives is "healthy" (or "good for you"), that vegetables are "healthy," or that your complexion is "healthy," she is using the word "healthy" analogously. "Healthy" means something different in each case, but there is a similarity among them that enables us to understand the relationship among all three. The medicine is healthy because it can, we hope, make us healthy; vegetables are healthy because they are a cause of health in the human body; a good complexion is healthy because it shows that the body is doing well.

Logicians and grammarians distinguish analogous names, like "healthy," from names or words that are called univocal or equivocal names. Univocal terms are those in which a name can be used of two different things but have the same meaning in both cases. Thus, we can say that David, Sarah, a lion, or a horse are all animals because they share in certain essential characteristics of what we mean by the name "animal": all are living; they eat, breathe, feel, and respond; they are self-ambulatory. We know what we mean when we say that all of them are animals. Animals as a class are different from trees, rocks, and the like—although given our contemporary culture and our sense of separation from other animals, the univocal nature of such a term may not be immediately obvious to us. We tend to use animals rather than identify ourselves with them!

An example of equivocation would be when we say that a dog is an animal, and that a human being whom we intensely dislike is an "animal." In the first case we are simply saying what the dog is—one who shares

with us in our animal nature. In the second case, however, we are saying that so-and-so is an "animal" because we find him gross and unattractive, his manners
are terrible, and he treats other people in an objection-
able way. Perhaps this second use of the term is unfair
to animals, but it is the way many of us talk. The term
"animal," in other words, has quite different meanings
in the two examples, even though the same word is
used.

Thus analogies, like metaphors, have a quite com-
monplace use in ordinary language. The difference is
that one uses images, the other concepts, but both
draw upon and arise out of our experience, and both
are important in describing and understanding our experience. But, as with metaphor, the problem with conceptual language becomes evident when it is used of
God. Analogy seeks to express and understand the relationship between us and God through the critical
and rational language we use about God. It seeks to
analyze the relationship between the eternal, transcendent God and finite creatures in much the same
way that one would attempt to analyze one's relationship with a person one knows—to understand the similarities and dissimilarities, what is like and unlike in
this relationship and any other. It is similar, or
analogous, to metaphor, but it differs in that it ab-
stracts our sense experience, which is usually expressed in images, in order to form ideas or concepts
about God.

Various concepts or conceptual names in the Christian tradition have been ascribed to God: good, just,
holy, true, person, one, unity, being—to name a few.
These concepts derive from our experience of the

world. We know to some degree what they mean when we use them of ourselves. When we say that a human being is "good," we are using the term "good" in reference to our experience, what our culture and training have taught us to believe about goodness. Or when we say a cause is "just," we are again reflecting certain standards and beliefs that have been formed in us.

But what meaning do they have when we use them of God? If we use such terms in a univocal sense, then we are saying that God is good or just in the same way we are good or our cause is just. We surely know, however, that our goodness and our sense of justice are very limited and fragile: we are always good with an admixture of what is not good; we are not good in an absolute sense, while no cause can be perfectly just for everyone. The current debate about abortion is a clear example. On the one hand, there is the right of an unborn child; on the other hand, there is the right of the mother. How are the two rights to be resolved in a way that is just and good for both? Therefore, we would not want to say that God is good and just in the same way we are, for that would be to confuse our limited goodness and sense of justice with the absolute goodness and justice of God.

Still, we would not want to say that there is absolutely no relation between our goodness and sense of justice and the goodness and justice of God. To say that would cut us off from any hope of sharing in what we believe to be the goodness and justice of God. As Christians it is our hope that finally we shall be able to share in God's goodness, and that even in this life the goodness we see in others is at least a glimpse of the eternal goodness of God. How many people have

been brought to belief in God, because they have seen
in another person a quality that has been for them a
sign of God's ultimate goodness? And many others
have been brought to a belief in God through their
struggle to create a more just society. However it may
be articulated, the struggle for the rights of others and
for oneself has its foundation in the belief that it is
grounded in something greater than we know in our
present experience.

Concepts about God, in other words, should be used
in neither a univocal nor equivocal manner. When they
are, they confuse the issue. Such univocal or equivocal
usage can lead us to think that God has no interest in
the human struggle for justice, or that our sense of
what is just is identical to God's. Equivocal language
denies there is any relation between God and us; univocal language identifies God with us and our concerns
in an absolute manner.

Analogy is another way of speaking about God. It
can enable us to say there is a relationship between
God and us that permits us to say certain things about
God without identifying what we say absolutely with
God. It makes possible language about God's goodness,
justice, and so forth, and it makes possible our understanding of God as the source of those qualities in ourselves. But at the same time it enables us to
understand that God's goodness, justice, and truth absolutely transcend what we know in our experience. It
can enable us to say that the good qualities we know
in our experience can give us at least an insight into
the eternal reality of God, a glimmer of what it means
absolutely to be good, or just, or true. Indeed, we
might say that it is those transcendent qualities in

God that help us to be good or just or true in a limited way in our own lives, and even more to share in them with God in eternal life.

Analogical language, then, attempts to express the relationship between God and the world. It says both what the relationship is like and what it is not like, and it reminds us to keep this distinction clearly in mind. Thus analogical language helps us to see more clearly the importance of the "negative moment" in speaking of God. As we have seen, one of the problems with metaphor is that it can easily lead us to confuse language about things in our experience with the reality of God to which the metaphor points—when we confuse God with our own parents, for example. And given the human tendency to confine God to our own definitions and concepts, analogical language has itself been misused in some theological systems. It can become an arbitrary and cold method that can easily become univocal—identifying *my* cause with God's cause.[8]

Some theologians have misunderstood the classical discussion of analogy in Thomas Aquinas, who is the chief exponent of this doctrine. For Aquinas, analogy has to do primarily with the language we use about God, but he stated clearly in his discussion of the names of God that we cannot confuse our language with the reality of God. All our language derives from, and is limited to, our experience of the world. Analogical language can no more define God's ultimate reality than can metaphor. The ultimate reality of God is always hidden from us.[9]

If we stop to think about it, language cannot actually define the ultimate reality of anything at all. It can only describe, point, or suggest; the rest is hidden. I cannot actually *be* another person; I cannot enter into the inner mystery of someone else, no matter how well I know that person. The language I use to describe my friend is always limited, analogical, expressing a relationship in which I think I know something, but not everything. This person is like me in many respects, but unlike me in others. We share many things, but we are not the same in other ways. The person we think we know best, and whom we think we can most clearly define and categorize in language, is often the one who can surprise us the most. The reason is that our best friends remain a mystery to us and can do or say things which are totally unexpected—that is one of the joys, as well as one of the pains, of friendship or marriage.

So too it is with God. God's mystery can be talked about. Our language points to it, but we cannot "put God into a box" any more than we can other people. The spouse whom one has loved for twenty years, the friend on whom one has relied for so long, can unexpectedly move in another direction. And just when we think we have everything worked out for our future, God can open up a new path for us. When that happens, we have to discover or be shown new language to talk about our relationship with God or with friends and spouses. We discover the "likeness and unlikeness" in the relationship that our previous language sought to describe.

The conceptual language of analogy, then, like the imagistic language of metaphor, directs us to the mystery of God. I think that nowhere in classical theology was this seen more clearly than in Thomas Aquinas's discussion of the most proper name of God: *Qui Est* or the One Who Is, Yahweh. His discussion shows clearly that our contemporary concern with the names of God is nothing new; it is central to the Christian understanding of God as ultimate mystery. The name *Qui Est* comes, of course, from Exodus 3: 13-14, where it is the central name for God in the Old Testament, the divine name revealed to Moses. Thomas cites three reasons why it is the most appropriate name for God, and those three reasons can direct us to a deeper appreciation of the significance of analogical language about God. The name expresses, first, God's way of existing; second, God's universality; and third, God's eternality. Those qualities in the name indicate the way in which God transcends the created order. They direct us to the mystery without defining it.

Certainly one of the most significant dimensions of Thomas's theology was his radical transformation of the meaning of Being. That transformation was important in the thirteenth century, because it enabled Christian philosophers and theologians to make creative use of the classical philosophy of Greece. It is significant for us today, as we rediscover a metaphysical philosophy and theology that concerns itself both with the transcendent and with the empirical sciences.[10] Thomas's fundamental insight into the meaning of Being was to understand it as the act of existence, *esse*, in Latin, which we would translate as "to be" or "to exist." The notion of Being, which is derived from Greek philosophy, has had a long history in Christian theology. It is now a term we use in the Nicene Creed to confess our belief that Jesus Christ is "of one being with the Father." It can be a static concept, a metaphysical first principle that obscures the dynamic nature of God expressed in the Hebrew name for God.

In Aquinas's theology, however, Being has a dynamic quality; it is the act of existing. For Aquinas the name "God" ought to be thought of as a verb, rather than as a noun or proper name; the name "God" means *to be*, the very act of existing. Therefore Yahweh, the name of God as the One Who Is, who says "I Am," expresses most truly God's absolute simplicity of existence. All created beings exist only by God's creative act. Our act of existence is derived from God. The name the One Who Is expresses that God is not, unlike all created beings, a determinate object that can be defined or given a name that would limit its reality. God is not an object of knowledge that we can name as we would another person. The One Who Is is the least determinate name we have to express God's reality as the simple act "to be."

Thomas is saying that the less we say about God the better, for the name of God is ultimately unsayable, a mystery hidden from us—somewhat like T. S. Eliot's cat. It is "a stammering, we echo the heights of God as best we can," he says, and he quotes John Damascene: "The first of all names to be used of God is [Qui Est], for he comprehends all in himself, he has his existence as an ocean of being, infinite and unlimited."[11] The God who simply *is* is an eternal present.

To speak in such a way of God is to speak analogically. To say that God *is* is in the most profound sense not to know what we are saying. We think we know what we mean when we say "I exist" or that another person exists, although I can perhaps be more certain of my own existence than I can be of another's; the latter could always be a dream or a fantasy. But I know that I exist as a finite creature, limited by time and space; I came into existence and I shall one day die. But God does not "exist" in such a way. To speak of God as "existing" is to use a word that has meaning in terms of my own experience, but can only point to God's manner of existence; it is a kind of "stammering," a straining of language. Yet it does convey some meaning. Just as we can say that God is good, or just, or true, we can say that God is, and have some idea of what we mean without knowing exactly *what* we mean.

Analogy, in other words, provides us with a way of talking about God that does not confuse our language about the world and ourselves with the incomprehensible God. It shows how our language leads us to mystery. As I said earlier, language is not just about facts or hard bits of data, but finds its richest expression in poetry and in its attempt to speak of what is inexpressible. In preaching, I have often been aware that I am struggling to say something that can only be contemplated in silence or communicated in non-linguistic ways—when I speak of the "love of God," for example. And yet we have to use language, even while recognizing its limitations. Analogy shows us the silence of mystery and the need for our silence in the presence of mystery. A name is spoken and heard, but it does not express to us all of the truth that can be known.

There is a well-known story about Thomas Aquinas towards the end of his life. Thomas was a prolific author, using several secretaries in order to write his commentaries on Scripture and Aristotle, as well as his compendiums of theology. It is said he could dictate to both his secretaries simultaneously, speaking to one about Aristotle and to another about the Bible. But at the end of his life, he became silent. He received a vision of Christ, and he is reported to have said that after what he had seen, all he had written was like straw, and he wrote no more.[12] That silence is a very good illustration of the silence towards which all language about God directs us. It can be a metaphor not only of Thomas' own theology, but of all theological language.

The story, however, should not be misunderstood; it was not a repudiation of the rational and systematic structure of his theology. Earlier in his life, in fact, before his vision, he had quoted favorably from St. Gregory the Great: "For however little he sees of the light of the creator, everything becomes empty to him."[13] Rather, it illustrates the silence that is the final meaning of all talking about God. As one writer has said,

> the silence [of Aquinas after his vision] is not the opposite of the words, but their true sense. We are to read the Summas with silence in mind, for the silence teaches us how to read the book. The greatest danger would be to listen to the questions of the Summa and not to hear the silence. Then one would hear only the outer rattle of Scholastic machinery. Then one would have straw indeed.[14]

The way of analogy, then, is a movement originating in the experience of the world and of ourselves. The language that results moves from that experience to the experience of God, where all language fails and we are simply in the presence of the divine reality. Reason, the natural knowledge of God, and our language about God find their end, when our knowledge of God is "a kind of experimental awareness...a knowing that, as it were, is tasted."[15]

CHAPTER VI
The Sacrament of Names

▪ 1 ▪

In this book we have looked at several aspects of naming the mystery of God. In earlier chapters, I sought to show how the Jewish and Christian naming of God began in the biblical tradition with Moses and Jesus. Both of those figures, so fundamental to Jewish and then to Christian belief about God, experienced the mystery of God in profound and radical ways. Moses, at the beginning of the religious history of Israel, experienced God as the one who could not be named but who simply *is*, the one who was heard in the silence of the burning bush and in the awesome power of Mt. Sinai. At the beginning of what was to become the Christian understanding of God, Jesus experienced God in more personal and intimate terms, as the one whom he could call Father, yet who has never been seen by anyone.

In the history of the church's life of prayer and worship, both of those names have been interpreted and amplified, as human beings have attempted to name the mystery with which they believe themselves to be in a profound and saving relationship. They have called God Lord, King, Master, the Holy One—all names suggesting transcendence and power. But they have also used names expressing a relationship of closeness and intimacy, especially in naming Jesus, who in the most radically personal way represented God to the writers of the New Testament—the shepherd who cares for his flock and seeks out those who are lost, the lover, the servant who washes the feet of his disciples, the woman who searches for the lost coin, the father who welcomes back his wayward son. The various names that have come to us in the New Testament and in the church's tradition of prayer and worship interpret the names revealed to us in the experience of Moses and Jesus. They show us how the naming of God results from the way we understand and make our own the names that arise from the continuing experience human beings have of God. Jesus showed his disciples new ways of understanding and naming the God of their ancestors both in what he did and taught, and in the new relationship he created between human beings and God.

Such names, as they arise out of the continuing experience of God, are names of power for those who believe. They allow us to see the connection between our experience of God in the present and that of believers in earlier generations. The God to whom we pray and whom we worship is a living God, one who is always being revealed in the new situations human beings face as they grow in an awareness of themselves and of the world. Many of the Christian names for God have their origin in God's revelation to the Jews, but they were given a distinctively Christian thrust, as the experience of God was opened up and expanded by the revelation of God in Jesus Christ, and in the continuing presence of the Holy Spirit to the Christian community.

Christian belief in the continuing presence of the Holy Spirit is a very good example of the process by which the early Christians experienced new depths in the reality of God. While the figure of the Spirit of God appears frequently in the Old Testament—the Spirit that breathes upon the waters at creation and inspires the judges and prophets—it is only in the New Testament that the Spirit is fundamentally related to God the Father and to Jesus Christ. Paul began the process of identifying the Spirit with the Father and with Jesus—a process that eventually lead to the Christian understanding of God as trinity of persons: Father, Son, and Holy Spirit.[1]

All names—whether names of God or the names we use for one another—arise out of our interpretation of the reality we are naming. Even those of us who name God out of the Christian tradition of Scripture and doctrine name a reality we have known in prayer and in corporate worship. And now, of course, as I suggested in an earlier chapter, new interpretations of the biblical names for God are essential as we western Christians reach out beyond the confines of our own culture and intellectual history. As we begin to recognize that the non-Christians and non-westerners we are seeking to reach have a history of their own, we will need to translate and interpret our concepts and names for God to different intellectual traditions.

Even in this culture, we have come to recognize that many of the names we use for God represent concepts quite foreign to those who have grown up in a world where the great biblical stories are unknown. Some years ago, a wealthy New Yorker offered to establish a zoo in Central Park containing cows and chickens, so that city children could see that milk and eggs did not come from cartons or cans. Christian teachers and preachers may soon be faced with a similar problem. The biblical stories that have shaped our naming of God—creation, the flood, the Exodus, and events in the life of Jesus—will need to be told in new ways, if they are to say something to us about God and the names that we use for God. If the biblical story of creation is forgotten or has never been heard, what will it mean to call God "Creator of heaven and Earth"?

Contemporary music and poetry may show us new ways of talking about the mystery of all that is—ways that are quite foreign to much of our hymnody and traditional piety. Some of those names arise out of sexual imagery that may seem quite bizarre to Christians who shy away from talking about their relationship with God in erotic terms. Our contemporary piety often leads us to forget or ignore the passion expressed in the writings of many mystics and poets. Love, whether for God or for another human being, gives rise to names that can express great longing and desire. As the often pale piety of the last century becomes less and less common in hymns and prayers, we may need to rediscover and develop more robust images of God, and those will affect the names we use to speak to God. The name "Father," no matter how great its revealed authority, still carries with it the image of the popular play and film of some years ago, *Father Knows Best*—a bumbling and not very bright tyrant in the household.

In addition, if we are concerned for the preservation and conservation of the natural order, then we can identify with Francis of Assisi when he speaks of God as being praised by brother sun, sister moon, sister water, brother fire, and mother earth. For Francis, these were not names of God, replacing the names given to us in Scripture, but they were certainly images expressing the relationship of the creation to God, and hence telling us a great deal about God. In a similar way, the Psalmist could speak of God as the one who sends a gracious rain, or who makes corn and wine and oil increase. Such imagery will always affect the way in which human beings name the God who is also revealed in the more austere names of Yahweh and Father.

As I argued in the previous chapter, one of the means for that necessary process of interpretation is the analysis of language as metaphor and analogy. Both can help us clarify what the names mean and how they are related to what we believe about God. When, for example, we speak of God as a friend rather than as a parent, we are expressing a relationship with God that is both metaphorical and analogical. The name "friend" is one Jesus used in the Gospel of John to speak of his disciples, and we can use it in much the same way when we speak of having friendship with God. We can compare our relationship with God to the one we have with our friends, just as we can compare our relationship with our biological parents to that which we have with God as our Parent—the one who brings us into existence and nurtures us. Friends care for each other out of choice, just as fathers and mothers care for their children out of their love as parents. But to believe in Jesus as the incarnation of God shows us the deeper meaning of the divine friendship and parenthood. Jesus in his life, death, and resurrection, in his being as a person, creates and manifests God's friendship and parental love for us. In Jesus, God chooses us and makes us friends with God and children of God. To put it somewhat differently, God can be compared to a friend or parent, but God is also our Friend and Parent by nature. That the nature of God is to be our Friend and Parent is made known to us in Jesus.

Jesus as the incarnation of God is both the metaphor and the analogy of God for us. As one writer has put it, Jesus is the "parable of God," because he is the one in whom the story of God's history with us is proclaimed.[2] A parable might be described as an analogy or metaphor in story form. Jesus often used parables in order to show what God is like and how it will be when God's Reign is fully established. In the story of the Good Samaritan, for example, the compassion and care of God and, consequently, how human beings ought to act towards one another, is announced through the medium of a story. What is abstract—compassion—is made concrete in the Samaritan.

Jesus, in a similar way, shows us concretely what God is like. But even more, on the cross he shows us the very nature of God: one who dies in order that others may live. The story of Jesus is the story of God in our history; he is the sacrament of God—an outward and visible sign of the gift God gives to us. Jesus in his earthly ministry was the outward and visible presence of God in our midst—a presence now continued in the sacraments of the church. He *is* the gift of God to us. It is his presence in our place of time and space that can enable us to see that all our names for God are sacramental, words pointing to the mystery of God and calling forth in us what we cannot express directly.

▪ 2 ▪

The names Christians use for God arise out of many different sources: Holy Scripture and doctrine, the tradition of prayer and worship, and the experience we have of ourselves and of the presence of God in our lives. Each is subject to interpretation and development. Even Scripture contains historical traditions that must be balanced and interpreted, one in the light of another. But the need to interpret and balance is seen most clearly in the tradition of prayer and worship that arises out of Christian experience and in the doctrinal formulations to which those traditions give rise. A rose by any other name may smell just as sweet, but the rose itself, and the names we use for it, evokes and calls forth different meanings. For one person it may call forth memories of romance, but for someone else a rose may be associated with death or illness—roses on a casket or roses in a hospital room. The roses are the same, but their meaning changes in different circumstances.

So too in forms of prayer and worship and in doctrinal formulations. People pray and worship differently, even those who use a common book of prayer. The language conveys different meanings to each person, and it calls up different experiences in the life of an individual. Perhaps the most obvious example is the word "sin." How many different meanings that simple word has for people! To some it may convey the anguish of struggling with pride, lust, and envy in one's life. To another person, however, it may mean something quite trivial, such as breaking a rule or telling "a white lie." Any good priest or pastor knows the care that must be exercised when using the word sin because of the different meanings the word can have for each individual.

In a similar way, the forms of worship can convey quite different meanings. As an adolescent I began to find the pattern of worship in one parish—a rather sterile form of Morning Prayer—inadequate to my experience of God, and I sought out a richer, more elaborate form of worship. The one did not invalidate the other, even though as a rather opinionated adolescent, I thought it did. Such differences, on a larger scale, appear throughout Christian history; Quakers believe in absolute simplicity in worship, whereas Catholics believe in a form of worship that speaks to all the senses.

Such differing forms of worship and the different meanings words have can give rise to different forms of doctrinal expression. For example, Lutherans have always placed great emphasis upon the doctrine of justification. They believe that our justification before God—our salvation or redemption—through the saving work of Christ shows us the nature of God as one who freely accepts us, not because of our merit but because of Christ's death upon the cross. Such a doctrinal position arose out of Luther's experience of salvation and his rejection of the Roman doctrine of merits and indulgences. The doctrine of justification—that human beings are both condemned and forgiven—has continued to shape and form Lutheran spirituality and, consequently, the language that Lutherans use about God—the God who is both wrathful and forgiving.

Roman Catholics, the Orthodox, and some Anglicans, on the other hand, while certainly not denying the doctrine of justification by grace through faith, have placed a greater emphasis upon the sacramental life as the means of salvation, and upon salvation itself as our participation in the life of God. At times in Christian history, especially at the time of the Reformation and Counter-Reformation, such different emphases were regarded as mutually exclusive. Now, in a more ecumenical age, we are able to see that such doctrinal differences complement one another; they are different but analogous expressions of the same faith in Jesus Christ. There is no one way to talk about Christian faith in Jesus Christ that excludes all other ways, nor is there only one way to speak about God. All of our names for God reflect how we experience salvation in Christ.

The New Testament itself reflects the beginning of a pluralism that has so enriched the Christian understanding of Jesus as the revelation of God to us. Paul, for example, talks about salvation in terms of our having been set free from the Law, so that we have nothing of which we can boast except God's free gift. He can, therefore, talk about Jesus in highly eschatological terms as one who is the prototype of the New Humanity, the new Adam, and so forth. Jesus is the sign and the fulfillment of our hope now, and of that peace with God that will be ours "in the last days." The Gospel of John, on the other hand, uses images of light and darkness and of our mystical incorporation into the body of Christ. Those differences are important, for they can shape and form how we shall talk about and name God.

If one has been shown the mystery of God and salvation through a life of participation in the sacrament of the eucharist, one will talk about God in a different way than will someone whose belief has been shaped primarily by the preaching of the doctrine of justification. The former will emphasize God's closeness to us and our "natural desire"[3] for God; the latter will emphasize God's distance from us—the God who is wholly other, but who is present to us in the proclaimed Word of justification. Each certainly is necessary, and each can be a corrective.[4] Each, however, represents a different spirituality, giving rise to different images and concepts about God.

Those differences in spirituality will also affect the way in which we understand the relationship of the past to the present and future. As I argued in an earlier chapter, there are essentially two ways of regarding the authority of Holy Scripture. On the one hand, its authority can be understood as final and unchangeable, no matter what changes may have occurred in our understanding of human nature. Such an attitude is evident today in discussions about human sexuality and the place of women in the ministry of the church. On the other hand, if Scripture is thought of as a continuing presence to the church within the context of the sacramental life, then it can be thought of as more open to interpretation.

As for the names we use for God, we believe God's reality is unchanging, but how *we* speak of the Holy One will to a considerable degree derive from the manner in which we have experienced God in our own lives. To understand the authority of Scripture within the context of a sacramental spirituality, a spirituality that finds its foundation in the presence of the incarnate Christ to his church, means that some emphases in Scripture can be modified and even changed, as the church continues to interpret Scripture and to understand how it speaks to a new situation. A sacramental spirituality has formed the way in which I, and many others in my tradition, understand our relationship to God.[5] It is a sacramental spirituality that derives from a particular way of understanding and believing in the incarnation of God in Christ. For the great majority of Christians, both those today and those in the past, belief in the Incarnation is central to their belief in Jesus Christ, no matter what their ecclesial tradition may be. The doctrine of the Incarnation, as it was finally formulated at the Council of Chalcedon in the fifth century, sought to define what Christians had already come to believe, namely, that in Jesus Christ there are two natures, divine and human, and that Jesus is truly God and truly Man, in one Person.[6] As we confess in the Nicene Creed, in Jesus Christ the eternal Son of God "came down from heaven; by the power of the Holy Spirit he became incarnate from the Virgin Mary, and was made man." Neither the Creed nor the Chalcedonian Definition expressed a "new" belief about Jesus. Both brought together and gave precise expression to what Christian people had come to believe through their participation in Christ and their experience of salvation in him through the working of the Spirit in their lives.

Because many of the philosophical presuppositions in the Creed and the Definition are unfamiliar to us, both need interpretation. We who have a much more expanded understanding of the cosmos, for example, may not understand what is meant by the image of "came down from heaven." The authors of the Creed and the Definition assumed that the planet Earth was at the center of the universe, so that "heaven," while not a physical place (they were not as naive as we sometimes think them to be), could be expressed through the image of "above."

Nor do we understand "nature" and "person" in the same way as the Greek Fathers. "Nature" for us usually means our physical environment. In the Greek philosophy that lay behind the Creed and the Definition, it had the more general, although equally ambiguous, meaning of the "being" or "reality" of something—such as we speak of human *nature*. Today "person" usually means a center of consciousness, an individual with a name and with a particular human identity, but in early Christian theology it also had a more general meaning. It could refer to any entity that had its own unique way of existing—a legal corporation, as well as a human being. Gradually, "person" took a deeper, more limited meaning in Christian theology, but the richness of the term, as we use it today, resulted from many factors—the development of individualism, a greater awareness of human freedom and responsibility, as well as the importance of "interpersonal relationships" in personal growth. Both terms have thus undergone considerable development and change in meaning since the patristic period. They are analogous terms, in the sense that they mean different but related realities in different contexts. God is, we say, personal, and we are persons who have a personal reality, but the concepts are not quite the same in each use.

And yet, at a deeper level, we can see that both the Creed and the Definition are not just verbal definitions. They are not merely expressing a doctrine about Christ, but also providing us with a way of talking about how God is related to us and to our human history. Both confess that we do not believe in a Being far off and removed from us, but in one who is present to us in Jesus Christ. The Incarnation, in other words, is a doctrinal expression of the fundamental relationship between God and us, an analogy through which we can interpret and understand our salvation in Christ and our world at every level of created being, both spiritual and material.[7] The fundamental conviction they express is that God is with us.

Let me explain what I mean by an example drawn from ordinary human experience. There are fundamentally two ways in which another person can be present in my life and a significant factor in the way I understand myself. In the past, I have had teachers who influenced me greatly, not only by what they taught, but even more by being the kind of people they were. In all probability I could not have become the kind of person I am without their influence. Consequently, I remember them as guides, mentors, and, in many ways, as those who redeemed me from some of my false starts and stupid ways. My gratitude towards them is very deep, and I will never forget them. I remember one such teacher who had faith in me when no one else did, not even myself. But in spite of the effect he had upon me, he remains a figure in my past, one whom I remember, yet who is present to me only as a memory.

On the other hand, there are friends who are present with me now, and whose influence is shaping my life and enabling me to become the kind of person I want to be and ought to be. Such a person—whether a close friend, or a wife or husband—is not simply a memory, but one whose influence is a daily fact. A good friend or a spouse can enter into my life, and I can enter into his or hers, to such a degree that we can talk about "participating" in one another's lives. We have *communion* with one another, a sense of fellowship and sharing that I cannot have with someone who is only a memory.

In the New Testament, the word *koinonia* is used to describe such a relationship. *Koinonia* expresses the close bond that can exist not only between human beings, but also between human beings and God. In Christ, 1 John says, we share together in a common life

In an analogous manner, the Incarnation can be understood in two ways. Some Christians certainly believe in and understand the Incarnation as a historical event that happened in the man Jesus at a particular time and place. Its importance is shown in the divine authority of the teaching of Jesus, and, most importantly, in the cross and resurrection. In the cross we are redeemed; our sins are wiped away; we are set free from bondage to sin and death. In the resurrection our redemption is confirmed, so that we can now live in the promise and hope of what was accomplished on the cross. For such a way of thinking, the importance of the Incarnation lies in its having been an event in the past that makes possible our redemption in the present—in much the way as a great teacher in the past can affect our lives now. In turn, the church is understood as a body called together to witness to our redemption in Christ and, through preaching the Word of God, to proclaim it to others who have not heard the good news. Thus, for some in the Protestant tradition, the church commemorates the saving deeds and authoritative teaching of Christ and witnesses to Jesus in the remembrance of what he has done for us.

There is, however, another way of believing in the Incarnation and understanding how it is related to human existence. It is to believe in the sacramental presence of Jesus now in the church. This other way certainly affirms the Incarnation as an historical event: it happened in Jesus of Nazareth. But for this way of thinking, the Incarnation has significance as well for our present life in the church and for our understanding of the cosmos itself. It understands the church as the continuing presence of God in Christ and the cosmos as the place where God is actively present in the eternal Word and Son. Just as another human being can be present to us now, and not merely a memory, so we believe Jesus the risen and exalted Lord is present to us now as the true presence of God.

Such a way of understanding and believing in the Incarnation had its origin in the Fourth Gospel, in which John frequently uses imagery of participation in the life of God. One example is Jesus' description of himself as the "true vine" to speak about his relationship with the disciples (John 15:1-8). Another example would be the High Priestly Prayer (John 15-16), where John lays the foundation for the later trinitarian doctrine about the relation between Jesus and the Father. And that in turn led Christians to see more deeply the union of all believers in Jesus with the Father—their participation in God because of their belief in Jesus. Indeed, Jesus was the sign of the communion of all human beings with God:

> I do not pray for these only, but also for those who believe in me through their word, that they may all be one; even as thou, Father, art in me, and I in thee, that they also may be in us, so that the world may believe that thou hast sent me. The glory which thou hast given me I have given to them, that they may be one even as we are one, I in them and thou in me, that they may become perfectly one (John 17:20-23).

This and many other passages in the Fourth Gospel were the beginning of the intellectual struggle by Christians in the early church between what they believed about Jesus and what they believed about the God whom he called Father. Was Jesus simply a preacher who taught his disciples a new way of life, or was he one with the God who created and governed the cosmos? And—even more importantly—can *we* through Jesus be one with the creator and governor of all things?

Justin Martyr, a pagan philosopher who was converted to Christianity in the second century, also sought to show how Jesus was the incarnation of the divine Word or Logos of God. That Word, incarnate in Jesus, made it possible to think of the presence of God in all human beings, so that even pagan philosophers such as Plato could understand something of the order and structure of the universe. What they had known only by anticipation was now fully made known in Jesus.

Subsequent patristic theology would develop this idea, seeking to show how Jesus as the incarnation of the second person of the Trinity could incorporate all humanity into himself. Because of the Incarnation, our human nature is taken up into God, incorporated into the divine nature by grace and hope. As one of the early theologians of the church said, Jesus is the Son of God by nature; in the Incarnation we are made the sons and daughters of God by adoption and grace. This theme was central to the development of the doctrine of the Incarnation throughout the patristic period, and with some modifications it persisted through the medieval period as well. It lies behind the doctrine of *theosis*, or divinization, a doctrine that has remained central in the life of prayer and worship of the Orthodox Church and in much of the sacramental theology of the Catholic tradition in the West.

The doctrine of *theosis* expresses the belief that human beings, while damaged by sin, nonetheless have a desire for union with God—a union that is fulfilled and completed by grace in Jesus Christ and through the indwelling of the Spirit in the believer. God in Christ and Spirit reaches out to human beings in order to bring them into union with God. God is not a figure afar off, and Jesus is not simply a figure in the past. Rather, through the indwelling presence of the Spirit we are called into communion with God the Trinity and conformed to Christ. Its emphasis is upon our present and future relationship with God as a hope or promise yet to be completed, but already begun. Because of the death, resurrection, and exaltation of Christ, and the sending of the Spirit, we now have communion with God, a personal relationship of love.

Although this understanding of the relationship between human beings and God dominated much western theology during the Middle Ages, in the Reformation period it was largely rejected. The reformers objected to the superstition that had grown up around the sacramental theology so closely related to belief in the communion of human beings with God. They found it necessary to emphasize the radical nature of human sin and our distance from God because of sin. But the earlier patristic and medieval emphasis still continued in much of Anglicanism. That emphasis is well expressed in the Prayer Book collect for the Second Sunday after Christmas: "O God, who wonderfully created, and yet more wonderfully restored, the dignity of human nature: Grant that we may share in the divine life of him who humbled himself to share our humanity, your Son Jesus Christ."

This classical doctrine of the Incarnation and its relationship to the sacramental life of Christians, can help us see what it means to speak of the sacramentality of names, especially those names we use to speak of and to the Divine Reality we call God.

■ 3 ■

Most Christians, especially those who come from a catholic tradition of theology and spirituality, when they hear the word "sacrament," think of the church sacraments of baptism and eucharist. But the word "sacrament" has a wider meaning. If we think of Christ as the incarnation of God in the world, we are also speaking of the way in which God chooses to be present in all of the created order. We can then speak of the world as open to the presence of God in many different ways—in the church sacraments of baptism and eucharist, of course, but also in all of those physical, historical forms through which we know the presence of God among us. In this sense, Jesus is the sacrament of God, because he enables us to see who God is and what God is like: a God who is present to us in the historic life of a human being. God's presence in Jesus can enable us to see all the ways in which God is present to us. As St. Augustine (interpreting Psalm 36) said, Christ is the Light by which we see light. He meant by this that, because of Christ, we can see God's presence in those various persons, situations, and events that show us what God is like.

Let me give an example of what I mean. Two people who are married, or who are very close friends, usually go about their day-to-day lives without thinking too much about the relationship they have. They eat together, share common experiences, and so forth. They do not, if they are wise, spend a great deal of time talking about "the relationship"; it is simply assumed to be central to their lives, and it does not have to be analyzed or renegotiated every moment. However, there are times when the nature of the relationship becomes heightened and its importance made explicit. The birth of a child, for instance, or an anniversary, or some difficult situation such as a serious illness, can lead a couple to become more explicitly aware of the importance of their relationship. Their mutual presence to one another—their love—is shown to them in that time of heightened awareness. They may celebrate with a festive dinner, or in a time of distress simply sit together in silence. Both actions are sacramental, for they draw human beings together in a deepened sense of their love for one another. That time, when love becomes explicit, is the light by which they are able to see the love they share with one another day after day.

For Christian people, that Light ultimately is Christ, the one through whom we are able to see the light which shines in our lives at all times. The Light of Christ for many Christian people is especially focused in the eucharist, the sacrament that makes explicit the grace of God present to us day by day, even when we do not recognize it. In the eucharist, Christians believe, the love or grace of God that is always present becomes a *holy* communion, and we have the awareness that God is present to us always—God, the one who is simply "there," illuminates every other area of life.

Of course, as all those who participate in the eucharist know only too well, such a moment of illumination does not happen every time we participate in the eucharist, anymore than it does in marriage or friendship. There can be long periods of dryness and inattention. But it is the regular and disciplined life of participation in the presence of God, just as with the awareness of the presence of another person whom we love, that can bring us to those times when the presence of God is most clear to us. Those times enable us to know God's presence in every other area. In those moments I am able to hand over my life to God's grace and care, and to know more deeply what communion with God is—the basic reality of my life both now and in the world to come.

But we must be careful here. Christian faith is not pantheistic. God as creator, redeemer, and sanctifier is always present to us, but God also infinitely transcends us. The doctrine of creation is as central to Christian faith as the doctrine of the Incarnation, because it is the confession that we are *not* God. Our union with God, our participation in God, is always by gift and promise; we cannot claim it as ours by right. Indeed, the corruption in sacramental theology at the end of the Middle Ages, that (to some degree) sparked the Reformation resulted from forgetting that our communion with God is not something magical that we can control or manipulate. We are creatures with whom God chooses to be present; this is shown to us in the Incarnation and the continuing presence of Christ by the Spirit in the sacramental life of the church. Jesus, as the sacrament of God, makes it possible for us to be in communion with God and with one another.

It is in such a sense that all names are sacramental; they define the relationship between us and God and among one another. Or, as I put it earlier, the divine names are analogous. They do not just point to similarities, as do metaphors, but express in human language the reality of the relationship between God and us. When we say "Jesus is Lord," we are saying something different than "Jesus is like a Lord." The former expresses a real relationship between Jesus and us, namely, that Jesus is savior, ruler, the one who guides and directs us, the one to whom we can turn for help and nurture. There is nothing either "masculine" or "feminine" about Jesus' presence in the relationship, as there would be if we were speaking in a metaphor. The name directs us to the relationship, not to lords and ladies.

Something similar is true for many alcoholics who receive the sacramental wine of the eucharist. They know it is wine; there is no question about the reality of its being alcohol. But because of what they believe about it, namely, that the wine is the sacramental blood of Christ, the wine carries with it a different set of meanings than those associated with the wine that they used to drink for other reasons. It is wine, but it is more than wine; the "more than" is what makes the difference.

In other words, the analogous names we use for God, like sacraments, are grounded in the Incarnation and in what the Incarnation says about the world and God. The Incarnation is the *real* relationship between God and us, not simply one of likeness and similarity. It is, as the Letter to the Ephesians states, the mystery of God's will, "according to his purpose which he set forth in Christ as a plan for the fulness of time, to unite all things in him, things in heaven and things on earth" (Eph. 1:9-10). The analogous names we use to speak of God direct us to the relationship itself, the one established in Christ.

Perhaps we can see this more clearly if we think of human names, that is, the names we use for one another, for they too are sacramental. They express the relationship, the analogy, we have with one another. I can use the name of another person in at least two ways. The name can simply be a way to identify one person as distinct from other people—like a name-tag. The use of the name carries with it no great significance; it simply signifies that this person is Michael and not Bill. In many cases it would be simpler to use a number in order to identify the person, and indeed in our contemporary society, people are frequently identified by numbers—social security numbers, drivers' license numbers—rather than by name. Numbers can be more accurate and convenient at times, but they are clearly not sacramental in character.

On the other hand, a name can express both a personal identity and a personal relationship. When two friends who have known one another for many years and shared much together use each others' names, the name refers to a history of involvement and love as well as a knowledge of the other person—what he or she likes and dislikes, feels and thinks about many things, believes about his or her place in the world. A name can carry with it a knowledge of another person that is deeper than one person can express directly about another; it carries with it a history of feelings and shared memories that language cannot express.

A name can also express a hope not yet known. In the Christian sacrament of baptism (and there are parallels in other religious traditions), when a child is given a name, it expresses how the child is known to God and what the child is called to become. "N., I baptize you in the Name of the Father, and of the Son, and of the Holy Spirit," the minister says, and names the person in the Name of another, thus establishing a relationship between them. When a man and woman marry, they take each other as husband and wife by name. The name conveys the hope that the relationship will continue to grow over many years. When I bid farewell to a friend who is dying, I am both recalling a history and expressing a hope for my friend's future life with God. A past history and a future hope are both conveyed in the names we use for other persons.

But no name, no matter how well we know the other person, can convey the total reality of that person. There is always that dimension of another human being that is hidden from us and known only to God. Everyone has secret hopes and fantasies; none of us is completely open and honest even with those who are closest to us. The reason for that secrecy is usually that we do not know ourselves well enough to be able to express what is hidden even from ourselves. I do not always know what I shall be, because I do not have absolute control over my future. I do not know what will happen next year that may crystallize my fantasies and open up a wholly new direction for my life. And that new direction could well startle those who know my name and who think they know me. The relationship conveyed by the name is real, but it can never be fully understood and expressed. There is always a "negative moment" in any relationship between human beings. Names both reveal and hide.

So also do sacraments, especially the two major Christian sacraments of baptism and eucharist. Water and bread and wine are real. They are what they are, and as such they bring with them a history of associations—water with which we are cleansed, the water we drink, the bread and wine that sustain and refresh us. But as sacramental elements they also carry with them the hiddenness of Christ, a real presence, that cannot be fully grasped or conveyed in words:

Word-made-flesh, true bread he maketh
By his word his Flesh to be,
Wine his Blood; when man partaketh,
Though his senses fail to see,
Faith alone, when sight forsaketh,
Shows true hearts the mystery.[9]

In the Incarnate Lord, there is both a revelation and a hiddenness that only faith can see. Jesus is, we believe, the God-Man. He was a human being who was known in the flesh, who could be touched and seen. He wept and he was thirsty. He experienced the agony of doubt and of physical and mental pain on the cross. There was no distinguishing mark on him to proclaim that he was also God. He did not, as a theology professor of mine used to say, walk around with a sign saying, "I am God." And if he had, who would have believed him? His divinity was as hidden from his disciples as it is from us, and yet by the eyes of faith we can see him as God incarnate, and by the ears of faith we can hear his authoritative word. As a consequence, we name him Lord, Savior, Messiah, Son of God, and Son of Man. Those names say who he is, and yet they hide from us the mystery of his relationship with the one whom he called Father. They convey the mystery of the Incarnation; they are sacraments of the presence of God with us.

The names we use for that ultimate mystery of all things present us with a more complex problem than do the names we use for one another, or even the names we use to speak of Jesus Christ. The reason for the complexity is simple to state: God does not enter into our experience as other people do, nor even as Jesus does. Our names for other people arise out of our experience of them in concrete ways—hearing them speak, seeing and touching them. And our names for Jesus, even though we cannot experience him as we can the friend who stands next to us, arise out of the daily contact with him his disciples had. The mental picture we have of Jesus—that he was handsome, masculine, bearded, and swarthy, as he is so often pictured in religious paintings—may be quite false; nonetheless we do have the feeling that he looked something like us. But we can have no such mental picture of God, for to have such a picture would distort the mystery we believe God to be. As the Psalmist said of the idolatry of his own time:

> Why should the heathen say,
> "Where then is their God?"
> Our God is in heaven;
> whatever he wills to do he does.
> Their idols are silver and gold,
> the work of human hands.
> They have mouths, but they cannot speak;
> eyes have they, but they cannot see;
> They have ears, but they cannot hear;
> noses, but they cannot smell;
> They have hands, but they cannot feel; feet, but they cannot walk;
> They make no sound with their throat.
> Those who make them are like them,
> and so are all who put their trust in them.
> (Ps. 115:2-8)

Some of our contemporary idols can also distort the mystery of the God who "wrapped darkness about him" and who "made dark waters and thick clouds his pavilion" (Ps. 18:12). It has not been unknown for extreme patriots to idolize a political figure as their God, such as Hitler, or a president of the United States. Clergy have sometimes been known to encourage, or at least not discourage, an identification of themselves with God. Male priests can do that with the image of God the Father; female priests may someday do it with God the Mother! No human being is free from the temptation to impose his or her agenda onto God. Idolatry is making God fit one's image—whether that be male or female, white or black, middle-class or poor, powerful or oppressed. There is no agenda-free image of God, and hence there is no agenda-free name for God.

In this complex area of naming God, the relationship between sacramentality and analogy is important. To say that the names of God are sacramental and analogous is to say that they arise from the experience of God as the unnamed source of all that is, as Being itself. But analogous names, like sacraments, always direct us away from the materiality of our names to the one who can only be named in silence. That is why Christ, as the sacrament of God, is the analogy of the relationship between God and creation. He is the one who, by being present to us in the limitedness of our created existence, always points or directs us beyond that limitedness to what transcends us. As the analogy of the relationship between God and us, Jesus Christ is both named and unnamed, known and unknown, the revelation of God to us, but also one in whom the mystery of God is hidden. He both fulfills and breaks open all of our ways of naming God.

Jesus Christ, then, as the analogy between God and us, the sacrament of God's presence with us, stands at the mid-point, the center of Christian belief about God and the world. He is the one who shows us God; he shows us who we are in our created humanity. Out of our relationship with him, we name God and God names us. Jesus allows us to speak of God, but he also leads us into silence before the mystery of God and of ourselves.

It is perhaps a truism to say that human beings, especially when they are teachers of theology, tend to say too much about God. The theological tradition is, it would sometimes seem, overwhelmed by discourses about the mystery of the Incarnation, and the mystery of the presence of Christ (and therefore of God) in the bread and wine of the eucharist. At the present time, with all of the rhetoric we hear about the language which we use for God, it might be well to remember the silence of prayer, the silence of eucharistic presence, and the silence of our own interior lives. The names of God call us into silence. That is what analogy is all about—a speaking that is not speaking, a knowing that is not knowing, a silence that is, as Gregory of Nyssa said, a "luminous darkness." Names are sacraments. When we name ourselves, or another person, or even when we name God, we are speaking of that which cannot ultimately be known.

We can see this truth in many of the stories about Jesus in the New Testament. During his earthly ministry, Jesus could be touched and seen and heard. He could be named. But there was always about him something of a mystery. The questions people in the gospels asked about him are important for us to remember when we think we know Jesus (or God) too well. What is his authority to speak as he does? Where does he come from? He is only a carpenter's son from Nazareth; we know his father and mother. Who is this man?

This sense of strangeness about Jesus is intensified in his resurrection. He appears suddenly in a locked room or on an open road. He can be touched, yet he cannot be held down. And in his exaltation he can no longer be seen at all; only the Spirit he sends now makes him known. We name him Jesus, but we too have to repeat the Gospel question: Who is this man whom we name? He is one with us, and yet he utterly transcends us, because he shares in both the divinity of God and our humanity.

Jesus directs us to God. His name—the name at which every knee must bow, as Paul says—is a sign or sacrament of God's presence with us. It is a name that calls us into silence before the mystery of God. When we reflect upon this dimension of the name of Jesus, we can perhaps see more deeply the significance of all our names for God. The two great names from Scripture—I Am and Father—are sacramental names, because they call us into silence before the mystery. So, too, are any other names we may use in prayer and worship. They can enable us to speak to or about God, while at the same time calling us to see that God utterly transcends every name. What is revealed to us in those names is that, at the heart of all that is—Being itself, reality, call it what we will—there exists a benevolence, a caring, what we attempt to express by the word Love. As all lovers know, there are times, even in this life, when the lover cannot any longer be named, when there can only be silence before so great a mystery.

In this book I have not argued for the validity of one name for God over another. But as Christian people engage in the sometimes painful, but also joyous, exploration of the names we use for God, my hope is that we shall remember the dangers implicit in our contemporary idolatries. Idolatry is making God in our own image. It is a temptation especially real for Christian people, because we believe in a God who took our human nature and entered the history of our createdness. We cannot flee to an unknown and nameless God, nor can we worship a God who is simply the kind of God we want the Holy One to be—a God made in our own image.

All of our categories, images, and concepts tell us something about God, but they do not limit the reality of the one to whom we pray, whom we worship, and about whom we speak. Paul Tillich once remarked that the Old Testament is the history of God's battle with idolatry. And God is still doing battle with our idolatries. God is the one who is always recalling us to the God who is to be worshiped with reverence and awe, for God is a "devouring fire" who will cleanse us from all our idolatries.

Endnotes

▪ Introduction ▪

1. T. S. Eliot, "The Naming of Cats" in *The Complete Poems and Plays: 1909-1950* (New York: Harcourt, Brace, and World, 1952).

2. For the various translations of "Yahweh" and the presumed origin of the name, see Exodus 3, notes to vv. 13-15 in the Revised Standard Version.

3. For example, see the remark referred to by Bolaji Idowu in *African Traditional Religion: A Definition* (Maryknoll, NY: Orbis, 1975): "How can the untutored Africans conceive of God...? How can this be...? Deity is a philosophical concept which savages are incapable of grasping." Cited in Benjamin Musoke-Lubega, "The Development of African Theology," an unpublished thesis in the Library of Nashotah House. I am grateful to this thesis for many insights into the development of Christianity in Africa.

   See also the writings of John S. Mbiti, W. E. Fasho-Luke, and John S. Pobee, theologians who illustrate the increasing awareness of African Christians of a theology indigenous to Africa and the African experience of God, rather than one dependent upon European and North American concepts and images.

   For similar developments in Asian theology,

see Daniel J. Adams, *Cross-Cultural Theology: Western Reflections in Asia* (Atlanta, GA: John Knox, 1987).

4. Roland M. Frye, "Language for God and Feminist Language: Problems and Perspectives" in *Reports from the Center of Theological Inquiry* #3, Princeton, NJ. For a less balanced and more polemical view, see William Oddie, *What Will Happen to God? Feminism and the Reconstruction of Christian Belief* (London: SPCK, 1984).

5. Elizabeth Achtemeier, "Female Language for God: Should the Church Adopt It?" in Donald G. Miller, ed., *The Hermeneutical Quest: Essays in Honor of James Luther Mays on his Sixty-fifth Birthday* (Allison Park, PA: Pickwick, 1986), p. 109.

6. Frye, "Language for God," p. 11.

7. Rosemary Radford Ruether, *Sexism and God-Talk: Toward a Feminist Theology* (Boston: Beacon, 1982) and Elizabeth Schüssler Fiorenza, *In Memory of Her: A Feminist Theological Reconstruction of Christian Origins* (New York: Crossroad, 1983).

8. Ruether, *Sexism and God-Talk*, p. 12.

9. Ibid., p. 19.

10. Ibid., p. 19.

11. Ibid., p. 20.

12. See, for example, the inclusive language translation of the Lectionary as well as the proposed al-

ternative liturgies for the Episcopal Church. Supplemental Liturgical Texts, Prayerbook Studies 30 (New York: Church Hymnal Corporation, 1989).

▪ Chapter I ▪

1. This story is told about A. O. Lovejoy, professor of philosophy at Johns Hopkins University, when he was being interrogated by a politician who wished to deny state funds to the university because he suspected the faculty of being communists. The interrogation took place in the 1950s during the anti-communist scare in the United States. Professor Lovejoy was especially well known for his scholarly work in the history of ideas.

2. See, for example, Peter Berger, *A Rumor of Angels* (New York: Doubleday, 1970).

3. Etienne Gilson, *God and Philosophy* (New Haven: Yale University Press, 1941).

4. For a lucid analysis of the problem of conceptual language about God and its necessity, see Gordon D. Kaufman, *The Theological Imagination: Constructing the Concept of God* (Philadelphia: Westminster, 1981).

5. Bernhard W. Anderson, *Understanding the Old Testament*, 4th ed. (Englewood Cliffs, NJ: Prentice-Hall, 1986), pp. 58ff.

6. *Ibid.*, p. 61.

7. See especially Isaiah 40-66. Cf. Anderson, *Understanding the Old Testament*, pp. 472ff.

8. Mary Daly, *Beyond God the Father* (Boston: Beacon, 1973) and *Gyn/Ecology* (Boston: Beacon, 1979). See also Judith Ochshorn, *The Female Experience and the Nature of the Divine* (Bloomington, IN: Indiana University Press, 1981).

9. See Robert Hammerton Kelly, *God the Father* (Philadelphia: Fortress, 1979); Walter Kasper, *The God of Jesus Christ*, trans. Matthew J. O'Connell (New York: Crossroad, 1984); Paul Ricoeur, *The Conflict of Interpretations* (Evanston, IL: Northwestern University Press, 1974).

10. Edward Schillebeeckx, *Jesus: An Experiment in Christology*, trans. Hubert Hoskins (New York: Crossroad, 1979), p. 268.

11. Kasper, *The God of Jesus Christ*, p. 132.

12. Biblical scholars question the authenticity of Matthew 28:18-20 as part of the original gospel. It is more probable that the divine commission and the trinitarian formula that it expresses were derived from the baptismal practice of the early church. But the fact remains that this baptismal formula was part of the received tradition.

13. J. B. Phillips, *Your God Is Too Small* (New York: Macmillan, 1961).

14. Such would seem to be the case in Karl Marx's judgment upon religious belief—that it contributed to the oppression of the workers. See,

however, Reinhold Niebuhr's introduction to *Karl Marx and Friedrich Engels: On Religion* (New York: Schocken Books, 1964).

15. See the argument of Sallie McFague that the traditional language for God has had an influence upon the way in which we think about and treat our environment. *Models of God: Theology for an Ecological, Nuclear Age* (Philadelphia: Fortress, 1987).

▪ Chapter II ▪

1. The Hymnal 1940 (451). In The Hymnal 1982 (670) the text was revised in order to be less offensive to contemporary sensibilities.

2. Amos could well be considered the "prophet of the word." Except for the recounting of his visions, the entire book consists of the words that Amos received from God.

3. For an analysis of the contrast and similarities between the biblical and Greek notions of truth, see Wolfhart Pannenberg, "Faith and Reason" in *Basic Questions in Theology*, vol. 2 (Philadelphia: Fortress, 1971).

4. In the patristic period, the earliest example of this desire to see the relationship between philosophy and Christian faith is that of Justin Martyr in the second century. I shall discuss Justin's contribution in a later chapter.

5. "It is impossible to come to the knowledge of the Trinity of divine persons through natural reason....Through natural reason man can know God only from creatures; and they lead to the knowledge of him as effects do to their cause. Therefore by natural reason we can know of God only what characterizes him necessarily as the source of all beings....Now the creative power of God is shared by the whole Trinity; hence it goes with the unity of nature, not with the distinction of persons. Therefore through natural reason we can know what has to do with the unity of nature, but not with the distinction of persons." *Summa Theologiae* (Blackfriars) 1a. II. 32, 1, *responsio*.

6. Because of various cultural, theological, and philosophical developments in the post-medieval period, the notion of faith changed dramatically. No longer did it mean accepting the received tradition of the church; it came to have a much more existential or personal meaning. Even in Calvin, for whom reason was still important, the rational analysis of the created order could not bring us to saving faith.

7. See, for example, two statements issued by authorities in the Roman Catholic Church: "The Declaration on the Admission of Women to the Ministerial Priesthood" (*Origins* 6:33) and the "Letter to the Bishops of the Catholic Church on the Pastoral Care of Homosexual Persons" issued by the Congregation for the Doctrine of the Faith (published in *The Tablet*, 8 November 1986). Both statements rest upon assumptions about biblical

authority that the Roman Catholic Church would find difficult to justify in other matters, e.g., the infallibility of the papal office or the bodily assumption of Mary. For another point of view on sexual ethics in particular, see L. William Countryman, *Dirt, Greed, and Sex: Sexual Ethics in the New Testament and Their Implications for Today* (Philadelphia: Fortress, 1988).

8. See the several discussions of authority in the church in the *Final Report* (London: SPCK, 1982) of the Anglican-Roman Catholic International Commission.

9. See the article by L. William Countryman, "The Gospel and the Institutions of the Church with Particular Reference to the Historic Episcopate," *Anglican Theological Review* 66 (October 1984):4.

10. Liberation theology is particularly concerned to develop the notion of *praxis*—Christian action in the world—as essential to Christian faith. For the classic discussion of this issue, see Gustavo Gutierrez, *A Theology of Liberation: History, Politics and Salvation* (Maryknoll, NY: Orbis, 1973). There have been many subsequent discussions of this matter, but Gutierrez is the source of them all.

11. For Anglicans, the discussion of the authority of Scripture and its interpretation by Richard Hooker in *The Laws of Ecclesiastical Polity* is still important. Hooker argued in Book 3:18 that Scripture is authoritative for us as we are able to

appropriate it through our rational interpretation of it.

12. Book of Common Prayer, p. 868.

13. See the form of the Apostles' Creed as it is now used in the baptismal service of the Book of Common Prayer.

14. *The Encyclopedia of Theology* s.v. "Tradition," by Karl-Heinz Weger.

■ Chapter III ■

1. A saying attributed to Evagrius the monk.

2. Feuerbach, from a philosophical point of view, and Freud, from a psychoanalytical one, each criticized the notion of God as a projection onto reality of human desires or fantasies and delusions. See Kasper, *The God of Jesus Christ*, ch. 2.

3. See G. W. H. Lampe, *God as Spirit* (Oxford: Clarendon, 1977).

4. Patricia Wilson-Kastner, *Faith, Feminism, and the Christ* (Philadelphia: Fortress, 1983), p. 133.

5. For an interesting discussion of the way in which language can hide as well as reveal, see George Steiner, *On Difficulty and Other Essays* (New York: Oxford University Press, 1978).

6. This phrase is derived from Karl Rahner and Johann B. Metz, *The Courage to Pray* (New York:

Crossroad, 1981). In the first section of the book, Metz analyzes the relationship between prayer and political action.

7. See Pss. 68 and 105, where the contrast is made between God's anger towards those who persecute Israel and God's care for the chosen people. See also the canticle "The Song of Moses" (from Exodus 15), which speaks of God as a mighty warrior who hurls the chariots of Pharaoh's army into the sea.

▪ Chapter IV ▪

1. In addition to the references in chapter 1, see also Alvin Kimel, "The Holy Trinity Meets Ashtoreth" in *Anglican Theological Review* 71 (Winter 1989):1.

2. The tradition of a "natural desire for God" in spite of our sinfulness begins in western theology with Augustine before his involvement in the Pelagian controversy. That tradition continued throughout much medieval theology, especially in Thomas Aquinas. For Augustine, see John Burnaby, *Amor Dei: A Study of the Religion of St. Augustine* (London: Hodder & Stoughton, 1938). For later theology see Henri de Lubac, *The Mystery of the Supernatural* (New York: Herder & Herder, 1967). The notion of a natural desire for God was denied by Luther and Calvin, who placed greater empha-

sis upon our separation from God because of our sinfulness.

3. "One more word and *teaching* what the world ought to be: Philosophy always arrives too late to do any such teaching. As the *thought* of the world, philosophy appears only in the period after actuality has been achieved and has completed its formative process....When philosophy paints its gray in gray, then a configuration of life has grown old, and cannot be rejuvenated by this gray in gray, but only understood; the Owl of Minerva takes flight only as the dusk begins to fall." G. W. F. Hegel in the Preface to the *Philosophy of Right*, trans. T. M. Knox (New York: Oxford University Press, 1967).

4. For the development of Anglican theology, the crucial work was *Lux Mundi: A Study in the Religion of the Incarnation*, edited by Charles Gore and first published in 1891. *Lux Mundi* sought to show how a theology of the Incarnation could enable Christians to accept the critical and scientific theories of the nineteenth century.

5. See Erik H. Erikson, *Young Man Luther: A Study in Psychoanalysis and History* (New York: Norton, 1958).

6. According to Ivo of Chartres, *Decretum* 7. 101-103 and Gratian, *Corpus Iuris Canonici* 1. 23. 29— both standard handbooks of canon law in the Middle Ages and in the Roman Catholic Church until recently—women were not allowed under any circumstances to teach men, and they were

totally forbidden to teach candidates for the priesthood, let alone priests. Only men ordained to the diaconate or priesthood might interpret Holy Scripture. That there were canons forbidding them to do so would suggest that even then women were teaching men in some capacity. Certainly St. Teresa did not refrain from doing so, although she was careful to express appropriate humility when she did. For this information I am indebted to Professor Wanda Cizewski of the Theology Department of Marquette University.

7. See John Boswell, *Christianity, Social Tolerance, and Homosexuality* (Chicago: University of Chicago Press, 1980).

8. Bernard of Clairvaux, *On the Song of Songs* and Teresa of Avila, *The Interior Castle* and *The Way of Perfection*. These works are available in various editions.

9. "The Ascent of Mount Carmel" in *The Collected Works of St. John of the Cross*, trans. Kieran Kavanaugh and Otilio Rodriques (Washington, DC: ICS Publications, 1970), p. 69.

10. Jacob Burckhardt, *The Civilization of the Renaissance in Italy*, trans. S. G. Middlemore (Oxford: Phaidon, 1945).

11. Mark Girouard, *Life in the English Country House: A Social and Architectural History* (New Haven: Yale University Press, 1978).

12. See the earlier quotation from Hegel concerning the Owl of Minerva.

13. Ernst Cassirer analyzed this shift in conscious-
    ness and our way of understanding the world in
    *Substance and Function and Einstein's Theory of
    Relativity* (New York: Dover, 1953).

14. The most recent translation is *Phenomenology of
    Spirit*, trans. A. V. Miller and J. N. Findlay (New
    York: Oxford University Press, 1977).

▪ Chapter V ▪

1. Aristotle *Poetics* 1457b.

2. For a thorough study of the concept of metaphor
   see Janice Martin Soskice, *Metaphor and Religious Language* (Oxford: Clarendon, 1985).

3. Walther Eichrodt, *Ezekiel: A Commentary*
   (Philadelphia: Westminster, 1970).

4. See my essay, "Theology and Pastoral Care" in
   James E. Griffiss, ed., *Anglican Theology and
   Pastoral Care* (Wilton CT: Morehouse Barlow,
   1985).

5. The Book of Common Prayer, p. 306.

6. Gordon Kaufman, "Models of God: Is Metaphor
   Enough?" in *Religion and Intellectual Life*
   5(Spring 1988):17.

7. See Arthur Peacocke, "Science and Theology: A
   Critical Realist Perspective" in *Religion and Intellectual Life* 5(Spring 1988):53. In his elaboration
   of a theory of critical realism in theology, com-

parable to that of the scientific disciplines, Peacocke writes: "The nature of our talk about God makes it essential for both the individual believer and for the community of believers to recognize that the way to the reality that God is should be followed in *both* its modes: the mediated, positive way, through the world and the revelation transmitted through the community; and the direct way of contemplation and silence.

"To speak of these as *ways* to the reality that is God is to remind us that, as with the critical realist stance with respect to science, so a critical realist position with respect to theology has also to emphasize that it is the *aim* of theology to tell as true a story as possible and it, too, must allow gradations in the degree of acceptance, in belief in the 'truth' of, theological propositions. Theology *aims* to depict the reality that is God but the theologian must be critically aware of the provisional nature of many of his claims."

8. A thorough study of the uses and abuses of analogical predication is David C. Burrell, *Analogy and Philosophical Language* (New Haven: Yale University Press, 1973). See also David Tracy, *The Analogical Imagination: Christian Theology and the Culture of Pluralism* (New York: Crossroad, 1981).

9. "The Christian is the true and the most radical skeptic. For if he really believes in the incomprehensibility of God, he is convinced that no individual truth is really true except in the process which necessarily belongs to its true essence, the

process in which the truth becomes a question which remains unanswered because it is asking about God and his incomprehensibility. The Christian, therefore, is also the one who comes to terms with that otherwise maddening experience in which (to formulate it with bad logic but in an accurate description) one can hold no opinion to be completely true and no opinion to be completely false. Anyone who is quick to find what was just said to be dumb and superficial should consider that in the method of opposing contradictories, a method with which one would be tempted to refute what was just said, the one alternative always works only with an empty 'no' and hence grasps into emptiness. This grasp, of course, is the first appearance of the incomprehensibility of God, is both challenge and grace to accept it, and in this acceptance to discover one's own incomprehensibility."—Karl Rahner, "Thomas Aquinas on the Incomprehensibility of God" in *Journal of Religion* 58(Supplement 1978):S125.

10. The regaining of a metaphysics of Being, after a long period of positivism in philosophy, can be seen in such diverse theologians as Keith Ward, John Macquarrie, Walter Kasper, and, of course, Karl Rahner. In the United States that process began with Paul Tillich, who stood over against the biblicism of most American theology.

11. Aquinas *Summa Theologiae* 1a, q. 13, art. 11.

12. For a discussion of the historical evidence and the theological significance of this vision and saying, see James A. Weisheipl, *Friar Thomas D'Aquino: His Life, Thought, and Work* (Garden City, NY: Doubleday, 1974).

13. Aquinas *Summa Theologiae* 2a 2ae, 180, 5, ad 3.

14. John D. Caputo, *Heidegger and Aquinas: An Essay on Overcoming Metaphysics* (New York: Fordham University Press, 1982), p. 256.

15. Aquinas *Summa Theologiae* 1a, 43, 5, ad. 2.

▪ Chapter VI ▪

1. The doxologies used by Paul in several of his letters indicate his growing awareness of the relationship between Jesus and the Spirit. The opening verses of Romans is a particularly good example. There he speaks of Jesus as the Son who was descended from David "according to the flesh" and "designated Son of God in power according to the Spirit of holiness by his resurrection" (Rom. 1:3-4).

2. Frederick Borsch, *God's Parable* (Philaadelphia: Fortress, 1975).

3. See, for instance, Peter Toon, *Justification and Sanctification* (Westchester, IL: Crossway Books, 1983) and Phillip E. Hughes, ed., *Faith and Works: Cranmer and Hooker on Justification* (Wilton, CT: Morehouse Barlow, 1982).

4. See the studies by de Lubac and Burnaby cited earlier.

5. *The Report of the Lutheran-Episcopal Dialogue*, 2nd series, 1976-1980 (Cincinnati, OH: Forward Movement, 1981).

6. See "Historical Documents of the Church" in the Book of Common Prayer, p. 864.

7. See Arthur R. Peacocke, "Theology and Science Today" in Ted Peters, ed., *Cosmos as Creation: Theology and Science in Consonance* (Nashville, TN: Abingdon Press, 1989).

8. *The Mystical Theology of the Eastern Church* (London: James Clarke, 1957), pp. 177 and 179.

9. Thomas Aquinas, *Pange Lingua*, The Hymnal 1940 (199).

Select Bibliography

Daniel J. Adams, *Cross Cultural Theology: Western Reflections in Asia* (Atlanta, GA: John Knox, 1987).

Bernhard W. Anderson, *Understanding the Old Testament*, 4th ed. (Englewood Cliffs, NJ: Prentice-Hall, 1986).

John Boswell, *Christianity, Social Tolerance, and Homosexuality* (Chicago: University of Chicago Press, 1980).

David C. Burrell, *Analogy and Philosophical Language* (New York and London: Yale University Press, 1973).

L. William Countryman, *Dirt, Greed, and Sex: Sexual Ethics in the New Testament and Their Implications for Today* (Philadelphia: Fortress, 1988).

Mary Daly, *Beyond God the Father* (Boston: Beacon, 1973).

Mary Daly, *Gyn/Ecology* (Boston: Beacon, 1979).

James E. Griffiss, ed., *Anglican Theology and Pastoral Care*, (Wilton, CT: Morehouse Barlow, 1985).

Walter Kasper, *The God of Jesus Christ*, trans. Matthew J. O'Connell (New York: Crossroad, 1984).

Gordon D. Kaufman, "Models of God: Is Metaphor Enough?" in *Religion and Intellectual Life*, Spring 1988, vol. V, No. 3.

Gordon D. Kaufman, *The Theological Imagination: Constructing the Concept of God* (Philadelphia: Westminster, 1981).

Robert Hammerton Kelly, *God the Father* (Philadelphia: Fortress Press, 1979).

Alvin Kimel, "The Holy Trinity Meets Ashtoreth" in *Anglican Theological Review* 71 (Winter 1989): 1.

Sallie McFague, *Models of God: Theology for an Ecological, Nuclear Age* (Philadelphia: Fortress, 1987).

Judith Ochshorn, *The Female Experience and the Nature of the Divine* (Bloomington: Indiana University Press, 1981).

Karl Rahner and Johann B. Metz, *The Courage to Pray* (New York: Crossroad, 1981).

Paul Ricoeur, *The Conflict of Interpretations* (Evanston, IL: Northwestern University Press, 1974).

Rosemary Radford Ruether, *Sexism and God-Talk: Toward a Feminist Theology* (Boston: Beacon, 1982).

Thomas Aquinas, *Summa Theologiae* (Blackfriars edition).

Edward Schillebeeckx, *Jesus: An Experiment in Christology*, trans. Hubert Hoskins (New York: Crossroad, 1979).

Elizabeth Schüssler Fiorenza, *In Memory of Her: A Feminist Theological Reconstruction of Christian Origins* (New York: Crossroad, 1983).

Janice Martin Soskice, *Metaphor and Religious Language* (Oxford: Clarendon Press, 1985).

David Tracy, *The Analogical Imagination: Christian Theology and the Culture of Pluralism*, (New York: Crossroad, 1981).

Patricia Wilson-Kastner, *Faith, Feminism, and the Christ* (Philadelphia: Fortress, 1983).

Index

D

Daly, Mary 28

dialectic 106 – 109

E

Elijah 24

Elohim 2, 25

Enlightenment 17, 21, 47

Ephesians, Letter to the 170

Episcopal Church 11, 52, 72

eucharist 61, 82, 102, 125 –
127, 158, 166 – 168, 170,
172, 176

Exodus 1, 18, 21, 24, 29, 44

experience
and community 112 – 113
as basis for theology 86-87,
92 – 93, 95 – 96, 109 –
110, 113
of God 86, 97, 109 – 110,
113 – 115, 150
personal 87, 93, 97 – 99,
108 – 109, 112, 114, 155
See also Hegel
See also Kant

Ezekiel, Book of 121

F

Father 4 – 6, 8, 12, 27 – 28, 31 –
38, 41, 43, 58, 62, 69 – 70,
78 – 81, 83, 85 – 86, 100,
115, 121, 134, 149, 151 –
153, 164, 173, 177

fatherhood
human 6, 28 – 30, 32, 122
of God 34, 36
used of God 29

Fourth Gospel 34, 163
See Gospel of John

Freud, Sigmund 28

Friend 83, 121, 128, 153 – 154

friendship 49, 71, 114, 171 –
172

Frye, Roland M. 8–9

G

Genesis, Book of 23

God
and Israel 8, 18, 24, 26, 29
– 31, 36, 53, 85, 107 –
108, 110
feminine imagery and 8 –
9, 16, 134
masculine language for 3,
7 – 10, 16, 48, 60, 69, 79,
81, 128, 134
mystery of 2 – 3, 15, 21–
22, 24, 26 – 28, 37, 39,
81 – 82, 126 – 127, 130 –
131, 133 – 134, 142 –
144, 149, 173, 175 – 177
personal relationship with
12, 16, 22, 31, 35, 49, 66
– 67, 70, 78 – 79, 87, 92,
100, 107 – 108, 114 –
115, 123, 128, 135, 152 –
153, 165 – 166
See also Abba; Adonai;
Being; Creator; Elohim;

Cowley Publications

is a ministry of the Society of St. John
the Evangelist, a religious community
for men in the Episcopal Church. Emerg-
ing from the Society's tradition of prayer,
theological reflection, and diversity of
mission, the press is centered in the rich
heritage of the Anglican Communion.

■

Cowley Publications seeks to provide
books, audio cassettes, and other resources for the ongoing theological exploration and spiritual development of
the Episcopal Church and other churches in the body of Christ. To this end, it is
dedicated to developing a new generation
of theological writers, encouraging them
to produce timely, creative, and stimulat-
ing publications of excellence, and
making these publications available
widely, reaching both clergy and lay persons.

About the Author

James E. Griffiss is author of several books, including *A Silent Path to God* (1980), *Church, Ministry, and Unity: A Divine Commission* (1983), and *Anglican Theology and Pastoral Care* (1985). Griffiss is former Professor of Systematic Theology at Nashotah House, and Visiting Professor of Systematic Theology at Church Divinity School of the Pacific.